John B. Keane is one of Ireland's most humorous authors and is recognised as a major Irish playwright. He has written many bestsellers including *A High Meadow, The Contractors, Durango, Inlaws and Outlaws, Letters of a Successful TD, Letters of an Irish Parish Priest, Letters of an Irish Publican, Letters of a Matchmaker, Letters of a Love-Hungry Farmer, Irish Short Stories, Love Bites and Other Stories, The Bodhrán Makers* and *Man of the Triple Name*. His plays include *The Field, The Year of the Hiker, Moll, Big Maggie, Sive, Many Young Men of Twenty, The Change in Mame Madden, Values* and *The Buds of Ballybunion*.

John B. Keane

SHARON'S GRAVE

THE CRAZY WALL

THE MAN FROM CLARE

New Revised Texts

Edited by
BEN BARNES

MERCIER PRESS

MERCIER PRESS
PO Box 5, 5 French Church Street, Cork
16 Hume Street, Dublin 2

© John B. Keane

ISBN 1 85635 100 9

10 9 8 7 6 5 4 3 2 1

A CIP record for this book is available from the British Library.

The Crazy Wall and *The Man from Clare*
are copyright plays and may not be performed without a licence.
Application for a licence for amateur performances must be made in
advance to Mercier Press Ltd., P.O. Box 5, 5 French Church Street, Cork.
Professional terms may be had from Mr John B. Keane, 37 William Street,
Listowel, Co. Kerry.

Sharon's Grave
is published by kind permission of Progress House (Publications) Ltd.
of 36 Home Farm Road, Dublin 9, Ireland, to whom all enquiries as to
performance of rights should be directed.

The Publishers gratefully acknowledge the financial assistance of
The Arts Council/An Chomhairle Ealaíon

Printed in Ireland by Colour Books Ltd.

Contents

SHARON'S GRAVE

Sharon's Grave was first produced at the Father Mathew Hall, Cork, on 1 February 1960, by the Southern Theatre Group, with the following cast:

Donal Conlee	Charles Ginnane
Peadar Minogue	Seamus Moynihan
Trassie Conlee	Maura Hassett
Neelus Conlee	Michael Twomey
Dinzie Conlee	Eamon Keane
Jack Conlee	Flor Dullea
Mague	Marie Twomey
Moll	Maire McLoughlin
Tom Shaun	Tom Vesey
Miss Dee	Kay Healy
Pats Bo Bwee	James N. Healy
PRODUCER	Dan Donovan
DESIGNER	Frank Sanquest

This new version of *Sharon's Grave* was first presented by The Gate Theatre on 25 July 1995 with the following cast:

Donal Conlee	Cecil Bell
Peadar Minogue	Stephen Hogan
Trassie Conlee	Catherine Byrne
Neelus Conlee	Brian O'Byrne
Dinzie Conlee	Mark O'Regan
Jack Conlee	Pat Kinevane
Miss Dee	Caroline Gray
Pats Bo Bwee	John Olohan
Chorus	Elizabeth Bracken
	Olivia Caffrey
	Amelia Crowley
	Eileen McCloskey
	Jennifer O'Dea
DIRECTOR	Ben Barnes
SET DESIGNER	Frank Conway
COSTUME DESIGNER	Jo Taylor
LIGHTING DESIGNER	Tina MacHugh

ACT ONE

Scene I

The action takes place in a bedroom in a small farmhouse on an isolated headland on the south-western seaboard of Ireland.

From the window, and through the open door, can be seen a dreary stretch of mountain, falling down to the sea. Crooked thorn-trees are everywhere along the mountainside and distant crags are evident also.

The room is poorly furnished. A large iron bed. An old iron washstand, in which a basin and ewer are deposited. A small wooden table, and hanging over the bed a large St Brigid's Cross.

An old man, emaciated, with white, scant hair, sits, propped by pillows, on the bed. He faces the audience. A bright quilt covers his lower body. In his hands a rosary beads rests. He would appear to be asleep.

The time is a late evening in March-ending, the year 1925. A knock is heard at the front door.

The man on the bed inclines his body barely, but does not otherwise heed the knock. The knock occurs secondly. A little louder. No movement from the old man on the bed. The latch on the door lifts and the door opens. Enter Peadar Minogue. He is a well-made man, 35 or so, with a weather-beaten copper-coloured face. He wears an old felt hat on his head, an old three-quarter length leather jacket and strong boots. His trouser-ends are tucked inside his rough socks. He carries a large satchel on his back.

For a while he looks at the form on the bed, and then peers closely at the old man ...

Peadar: *(Tentatively)* In pardon to you, sir. Could I disturb you?

(The old man does not move)

If you're asleep, sir, I won't wake you. Maybe you're only dozing and you might hear me. I'm looking for directions. *(Looks around room)* Maybe I'm in the right house, but I don't know. *(Doubtfully, to himself)* I shouldn't be here if 'tis the wrong house, disturbing people in their privacy, stealing into a place and witnessing things not meant for me. *(Then, kindly, to the old man)* Sleep your good sleep, old man.

(The old man stirs but barely, and inclines his head to

Peadar, who bends near him. The old man moans a little, tries to convey something, fails, and is still again)

Would you be sick now, by any chance, and not be able to dress your thoughts in words? I don't know! *(Turns and surveys the room again)* If you're sick, there will be somebody attending to you before we're older. I hope it isn't sick you are but asleep. I hope somebody comes in. I'll bide my time. They'll hardly turn me away. *(Takes off his satchel, places it on the floor, tiptoes to the window, peers out)* No sign of a being or animal to be seen!

(Peadar turns from the window, goes to the door, opens it and looks out, and stands a while in thought, looking into the distance. As he stands thus, a woman enters, silently, from the left. She is dressed in a dark frock, covered by a sacking apron, and wears strong boots. A cloth is tied tightly about her hair. She carries a bunch of daffodils in one hand and a short-stemmed earthenware vase in the other. She is slightly startled and looks in perplexity at Peadar, who does not see her. She makes a sound and Peadar wheels suddenly and looks at her, sweeping off his hat and clutching it in his hands. The woman is Trassie Conlee, thirtyish, of good carriage)

Trassie: Who are you?

Peadar: My name is Peadar Minogue.

Trassie: Peadar Minogue! There are no Minogues in these parts.

Peadar: I am not from these parts. Is this the townland of Baltavinn?

Trassie: It is!

Peadar: Would this, by any chance, be the house of Donal Conlee?

Trassie: It is. That's Donal Conlee there in the bed.

Peadar: *(Looks at Donal)* It's a strange thing to see a door leading into a bedroom, a door any man might walk in from the road.

Trassie: There were two holdings here in time gone. There are two doors still. We often thought to close one.

Peadar: Who are you?

Trassie: I am Trassie Conlee, his daughter *(Indicating bed)*. He isn't well.

Peadar: I thought he might be sick.

Trassie: Would you sit down?

Peadar: Thanks, I will. *(Closes door)* There is a fall of ground the whole way from here to the sea, I saw from the door. A healthy place and a wholesome place to live in. There is no air like the sea air.

Trassie: You can hear the sea here all of the time while there is quietness; at night above all. The sea is all around you. We live on a headland here.

Peadar: I saw that from the rise of ground. Not many houses hereabouts?

(Peadar circles and sits on a chair at the left of the bed. Trassie places flowers in a vase and places the vase on a table)

Trassie: *(Notices satchel)* Did you come far today?

Peadar: From Carraig Head.

Trassie: A good journey. You must have business in these parts?

Peadar: I'm a journeyman thatcher. I heard there were houses in the townland of Baltavinn that needed thatching.

Trassie: It's early in the year now for thatching.

Peadar: Work is hard to come by. No harm to try here for it. I saw the thatch of this house from the road. 'Tis rotting in every quarter. I heard in the next townland – Roseerin, I think they call it – that I would find a few day's work in the house of

Donal Conlee. They never said a word about there being sickness in the house.

Trassie: They'll never say that! 'Twas a pity you came so far with a false account. Anyway, while you're here, you'll drink tea.

Peadar: No ... No ... Don't bother yourself ... you have enough to think of ...

Trassie: I would be making it, anyway. I have a brother – Neelus; he is carting seaweed with the pony.

Peadar: It's good to have somebody in the house with you, especially with sickness.

Trassie: Did they tell you in Roseerin about him?

Peadar: Your brother?

Trassie: Yes, my brother.

Peadar: No word of him. His name was not drawn down one way or the other.

Trassie: Did they say anything about me?

Peadar: No! *(Significantly)* Only that the house of Donal Conlee would fall if it wasn't thatched.

Trassie: *(Smiling)* Looking for custom are you?

Peadar: Only what they said. *(Smiles)* A man in search of work will go all roads to come by it.

Trassie: What did they say about my brother Neelus?

Peadar: *(Smiles faintly)* There was no mention of him. Why do you ask the second time?

Trassie: *(Re-arranging the clothes on the bed, hesitantly)* Neelus is strange. He is a good worker – a great worker, but he is a small bit strange. People here in Baltavinn are saying he thinks of nothing but women, day in, day out; nothing but women! They do not know he is kind and gentle and they do not know he will wash the ware for me after the meals and make the beds. All they say is that he is mad for women! Which is a lie for them.

Peadar: Are there no women in Baltavinn?

Trassie: *(Surprised)* There are no girls here, only myself.

Peadar: Are there many men?

Trassie: Only a few, but all would marry if they could. There are no women of my age here. The famine swept most of 'em years ago and the ships took the rest.

Peadar: *(Indicating the old man)* What sickness has he?

Trassie: The heart! Three different attacks he has put over him. He was anointed yesterday by the priest. The doctor said there was only a little life left in him.

Peadar: What did the priest say?

Trassie: That he was not long for this world – to expect it any minute.

Peadar: The tag of death is on all of us. *(Sympathetically)* He looks to be a good age. A life lived out is no loss much.

Trassie: No loss to you.

Peadar: True. *(There is silence between them)*

Trassie: Is there anything else you do but thatch?

Peadar: I will do any work that will give me a good diet, a fire to warm by, and a bed to sleep in.

Trassie: Are you a married man?

Peadar: No! Travelling from one parish to another – no woman wants a man who won't sit still.

Trassie: *(Listening attitude)* That's Neelus putting the pony in.

         (Peadar rises)

Trassie: Stay sitting, let you. There is no harm in him only
         foolishness. Stay sitting and don't be put astray by what he
         tells you. I'll put your bag out of the way.

         *(Trassie takes the bag and exits left with it. Peadar surveys
         the man in the bed, rises, and looks out the window curi-
         ously. Enter Trassie)*

Trassie: Why are you looking out?

Peadar: No harm intended ... *(Doubtfully)* If I should go, tell me!

Trassie: Wait and have tea. Sit down, or he will be asking questions
         about you. Surely you will have a mouthful of tea and a
         forkful of meat cold before you go. *(Suggestive)* Or maybe
         'tis how you're afraid of things you do not meet every day.

Peadar: I'm not afraid, but I would hate to be the cause of upsetting
         the house by staying a while.

Trassie: There is no fear you will do that, but a sweet plate of bacon
         would give you heart for your journey.

Peadar: You make me feel hungry. *(Pause)* Does he know his father
         is bad?

Trassie: In his own way. A different way from ours, but he knows.
         He knows something is wrong. He is worried from that.

Peadar: *(Nods his head understanding)* Did he ever give you
         trouble?

Trassie: Not him! He is always helpful. Anything I tell him do, he
         will do. *(Worried)* Not him, but others are always making
         trouble.

         (Peadar looks at her for a spell and returns to his chair)

Trassie: *(Change of tone)* Of a Sunday Neelus will go down to

Carraig Head and go in hiding about the cliffs. He will spend his day watching the sea. If the sea is wild and making noise, he will come home deaf and you might as well be idle as to try and talk to him. If the sea is resting, he will come home saying things to himself ... strange things. *(Awkwardly)* He talks of the wind and the sea and Sharon's grave ...

Peadar: *(Solemnly)* Some men are like that from thinking too much about women.

(Peadar stirs nervously in his chair. Enter Neelus Conlee from the left. He is twentyish, dressed in tattered smock and waders. He has a vacant look, yet is handsome and refined of face. He looks puzzled when he sees Peadar)

Trassie: This is Peadar Minogue, Neelus. He was passing the road and he called, asking the way ...

Neelus: *(Smiling)* Peadar Minogue ... Trassie ...

(Trassie looks hopefully at Peadar)

Peadar: Very happy to meet you.

Neelus: *(Shakes hands with Peadar)* Pleased the same.

Peadar: *(Tentatively)* I heard good things about you.

Neelus: *(Suspicious)* Where did you hear them?

Peadar: Oh, lots of places ... Glounsharoon and Coilbwee and Kilbaha. Everywhere you could imagine.

Neelus: *(Hurtfully)* What used they be saying about me?

Peadar: Oh, you know the way people do be?

Neelus: Used they be telling you about me and the women? *(Peadar looks doubtfully at Trassie)*

Trassie: I'll lay the table for the tea. *(Moves towards the left, then loudly to Neelus)* If he wakes, call me.

(Exit Trassie. Neelus moves closer to Peadar)

Neelus: Go on about the women.

Peadar: *(Doubtfully, delicately)* They were saying you were a gifted hand with the ladies.

Neelus: Were they telling you about me and Sharon with her golden hair? *(Cautiously)* And Shíofra, the little vixen, with her face like the storm?

Peadar: *(Thoughtfully, weighing up Neelus)* It seems to come to me that I heard talks of you and these women you mention. *(Sureness)* Yes, I heard tell of it in several places. Yes, I'm sure now I did.

Neelus: They don't believe it, you know – a lot of them. They do be laughing at me, especially the girls in the mainland when we go to the chapel on a Sunday. I've seen them pointing me out *(Cautiously)* and I've heard giggling and whispering. Sharon has beautiful hair, red and golden like the sunset *(Elaborates with his hands)* shining like the summer sea and her skin as white as new milk and her voice is rich and deep and sweeter than the voice of a thrush. You never saw her golden hair?

Peadar: No, I never saw her golden hair but I have heard of it. Of course I know the way a girl's hair is and I can imagine what Sharon's would be like.

Neelus: *(Shrewdly)* What did you hear about it?

Peadar: I have forgotten most of it but I remember to hear it was brighter than gold.

(Neelus studies him suspiciously, and is then apparently satisfied)

Neelus: Shíofra is a little demon.

Peadar: Shíofra?

Neelus: Did you see Sharon's grave when you were coming here?

Peadar: No.

Neelus: *(Looks about cautiously and confides to Peadar)* Did you not hear of it?

Peadar: *(Interested)* What about it?

Neelus: *(Withdrawing a little – astonished)* You never heard tell of Sharon's grave?

(There is a distant look about him and awe in his voice)

It's a great deep hole over there on the cliffs. There is no bottom to it. It sinks down into the middle of the earth and water is always wild and wilful in it, even when the rest of the sea is calm.

Peadar: Why is it called Sharon's grave?

Neelus: *(Suddenly brought back to reality, eager to relate his obsession)* Sharon was a young princess of ancient times. Her father was a powerful chieftain in the county of Tyrconnell in the North country. Sharon was gentler than a doe and sweeter than wild honey. Her wild hair fell down over her white shoulders like a golden cape. *(Looks out the window, a sad note in his voice)* Sharon was travelling on horseback to the rich country of the Maharees down the coast. She was being married to a handsome chieftain with far lands and a tall castle rising over the sea ... *(He pauses)*

Peadar: Go on! What's the rest of the story?

Neelus: Shíofra was the name of Sharon's handmaiden. She was swarthy and humped and ugly and jealous of Sharon because Sharon was so beautiful. She poisoned the warriors of Sharon's father and there was no one left to help poor Sharon *(Reflective sadness)*, poor beautiful Sharon, and the old people say that Shíofra whispered a spell in the horse's ear when they were passing the great hole down below and the animal reared and jumped into the hole with Sharon upon its back ...

Peadar: Shíofra was an evil creature! Did she wed the young chieftain herself?

Neelus: Oh, no, indeed! *(Shakes his head)* No – no, indeed, she did not, for, as the horse was about to fall into the hole, Sharon made one last attempt to save herself and her fingers seized on Shíofra's girdle and she carried the wicked woman with her.

Peadar: And that is why they call it Sharon's grave?

Neelus: That is why! But there is more to the story. The old people say ... *(Looks about him as if he found somebody were listening)*

Peadar: Go on, Neelus. What do the old people say?

Neelus: The old people say that what you would think to be the wind crying is the sweet voice of lovely Sharon crying for her handsome young chieftain. They say that what you would think to be the wind blowing is the voice of Shíofra wailing and cursing in her misery.

Peadar: It is a sad story.

Neelus: *(Lonely)* It will be the same story always unless the bodies of two young men are cast into the hole. One will be small and ugly and wicked and the other will be tall and straight and pure like the noble chieftain.

Peadar: Is that part of the legend?

Neelus: 'Tis all in the story ... *(Turns to his father)* He's very bad ... my poor father, my poor father!

Peadar: With the fine days coming now, he'll improve. The fine weather is a great cure for all forms of sickness.

Neelus: *(Looks at Peadar vaguely)* The Banshee was crying last night over Baltavinn. I know the cry of the Banshee because it makes you shiver as if the cry was inside your ear. The last time the cry was heard, my mother died a few days after. God grant her a silver bed in heaven, my poor mother. *(Looks at his father)* He's that sick he doesn't know who are here and he doesn't know we are talking about him. That's very like death, that sickness.

Peadar: He's a long ways from being dead, Neelus.

Neelus: Did you ever hear the way Sharon cries in her grave in the quiet nights of summer?

Peadar: *(Doubtfully)* No!

Neelus: *(Cups his hands over his mouth and makes a whistling sound. Long drawn out and eerie. In the bed the old man stirs and moans faintly. In a panic, Neelus rushes to the left exit and calls loudly)* He cried out. Trassie! He stirred himself. He gave a moan out of him.

(Peadar rises and stands anxiously. Enter Trassie. She hurries to the bed and bends over the old man. She takes his hand and feels his brow. Then she turns to Peadar)

Trassie: It was nothing. The same as always. He is very weak in himself. He calls from time to time.

Peadar: Is he long ailing?

Trassie: This long time now. He got a fit a year ago. They said it was a stroke. He never rose from the bed since he took sick. This last week or so he is going from worse to worse. There isn't much a body can do.

Peadar: Is there no hope for him?

Trassie: He is too old to fight now!

Neelus: *(Draws near the bed, places his hand on his father's hand)* 'Tis when we'll all be asleep he'll go, the Lord save us! With no one to be near him. He'll be alone when he'll be called away into the caves *(Tone of awe)* and he'll be walking for ever and ever through the caves and he won't know where he's going and he'll be for ever and ever going deep down into the roundy caves and he'll never ...

Trassie: *(Gently)* Don't talk like that, Neelus. You know what will happen if you'll be talking like that. You'll be crying again and you won't be able to sleep. Stop it now, Neelus!

Neelus: *(Dejected tone)* 'Tis in the dark he'll come. Oh, he'll come like a fox and he'll sweep him away in a flash, my poor father.

Trassie: *(Firmly, gently)* Neelus, stop will you? You'll make trouble for all of us. *(Puts her hand around his shoulders)* Go down to the kitchen and wet the tea. The kettle is boiling. Go on now, Neelus a chroidhe. *(She gently manoeuvres him towards left exit)* You're a gift for making tea. *(She exits Neelus)*

Trassie: *(To Peadar)* What was he saying to you?

Peadar: Nothing you'd bother to carry with you.

Trassie: You needn't tell me. He talks of nothing else. He is a good-looking boy, a fine grádhbhar young fellow and the girls did take to him and they used to go with him, but somehow they run away from him now.

Peadar: I understand.

Trassie: I'm not denying he's a bit odd. But he was better than he is now.

Peadar: It's all right. I know what it is with him. No fault of his, the poor boy.

Trassie: Will you come to the kitchen and eat something now? You'll want something for the cold road.

Peadar: If you like me to, I'll sit a while and keep an eye on the old man. I don't mind. Many is the time I sat up with my own father when he was ailing ... I could stay. I wouldn't mind.

Trassie: *(Quickly, fearfully)* No! ... No! No need for you! Come to the kitchen. I'll stay here.

Peadar: Sorry if I am making too free. I meant well.

Trassie:	And sorry myself to think I refused your kindness. But his people will be here shortly. *(Hesitantly)* They might take offence if they thought a stranger was attending him.
Peadar:	You have somebody to relieve you, then?
Trassie:	I have.
Peadar:	Are they the one drop of blood?
Trassie:	His brother's two sons, my first cousins. They come here every night, about this time, to see him.
Peadar:	That's a pleasant thing to hear. That you have your own near you, when you want them.

(Trassie frowns a little. Peadar, puzzled, looks at her)

Peadar:	When there is sickness in a house, your own will be the first to help you.
Trassie:	You should be thinking of putting something in your stomach. Neelus forgets to keep the teapot warm.
Peadar:	There was no need to go to so much trouble for me. *(Rises)* In pardon to you I'll go down, then.

(Exit Peadar. Trassie seems to be about to call him back, but hesitates and folds her arms, worried. She tends to her father's comfort, leaves him and looks out the window, biting her lips, clutching her waist with her arms, pondering, turns, pats her father's forehead, waits a moment, and exits left, leaving the door but barely open. There is a sound of movement outside the front door. Very slowly the latch lifts and the door is pushed inward but nobody appears. After a few seconds what seems like a man with two heads appears in the doorway. They are two people, one carrying the other on his back. The man on the back moves and looks craftily over the other's shoulder, watching for movement in the room. The other looks stupidly about. The man on the back is Dinzie Conlee. The man carrying him is his brother Jack Conlee.

Dinzie Conlee is of indeterminate age. His face is

gruesome, twisted, as he looks about. He is slightly humped. A wizened small person, his legs paralysed.

The man Jack Conlee, on the other hand, is a large well-cut, well-proportioned man in his early twenties)

Dinzie: *(As he looks about)* Bring us in, Jack. Bring us in, boy! *(Gives Jack a prod in the back)*

Jack: *(Wincing)* Go aisy, Dinzie, can't you? ... Go aisy! You're always hurting me.

Dinzie: *(Ignoring Jack's feelings, goads him to the centre of the kitchen)* No one in, Jack! No one in! *(He surveys the old man)*

Jack: Trassie is out, Dinzie.

Dinzie: *(Always careful to ignore Jack's feelings)* Take us a-near the bed, Jack boy. Take us a-near the bed.

(Dutifully, Jack carries him to the bed. Dinzie leans over Jack's shoulder and surveys the old man)

Dinzie: Are you listening, Donal? ... Are you listening? ... *(Prods Jack)* Straighten, Jack! Straighten! You'll have me inside in the bed with him next. Are you paying heed, Donal? Wouldn't you die for yourself, wouldn't you? *(In anger)* Wouldn't you die, you old ropaire and not be keeping God waiting? *(To Jack, chuckling)* Maybe 'tis the Devil that's waiting for him.

Jack: *(Pleading)* Ah, don't, Dinzie, Don't! Leave him alone. He's our uncle!

Dinzie: *(Prods Jack on the back, and slaps the back of Jack's head so that Jack squirms)* On the table, Jack, boy. On the table. Or would you like to fly to the moon with me, and back? *(Chuckles)* On the table, Jack. Steady the blood! Woe, Pony!

(Jack backs Dinzie towards the table and puts him sitting on it, relieved of the weight, exercises his shoulder muscles, and approaches the bed to survey his uncle. Jack lies on floor and kicks his legs in the air like a horse. He snorts and

whinnies before he rises)

Jack: Will he last long, Dinzie?

Dinzie: *(Shrewdly)* It can't be soon enough for me, Jack! Frightful blackguarding, keeping the whole country waiting. He's holding on for spite, Jack.

Jack: *(Pleads)* Ah, Dinzie, he's our uncle. 'Tisn't right to talk like that.

Dinzie: *(Shouts at the man in the bed)* Wouldn't you die for yourself and not be keeping us all dancing attendance on you?

(Enter Trassie from left)

Trassie: I heard the voices. I knew who it was. I was getting the tea.

Dinzie: Wouldn't you have a word of welcome for us, anyway? We aren't soupers!

Trassie: *(Pleasantly)* I'm sorry if I sounded the way you said, especially when ye come here every evening to see him.

Dinzie: *(Sanctimoniously)* There's no harm in us. We praises everyone as we go along. We keeps to ourselves. Don't we, Jack? ... I say, don't we Jack?

Jack: We do, Dinzie, we do.

Trassie: *(Indicating bed)* He's not good this evening.

Dinzie: We was praying all night for him. Jack said a pile of prayers, too. Didn't you, Jack? You should have heard Jack praying. His guts rumbles when he says his prayers. I say, didn't you, Jack?

Jack: Oh, I did! I did!

Trassie: Would you like a drop of tea?

Dinzie: You know it wasn't the tea that brought us, Trassie! I'm the kind of man that if I wanted tea, I'd ask up. We're not oul'

women, Trassie. We never drink tea, except for our breakfast and supper.

Trassie: What brought you so?

Dinzie: Ah, now, Trassie, don't be trickin' with your own cousin.
You know the thing we were talking about, don't you?

Trassie: *(Hotly)* I told you before, Dinzie Conlee, that I wouldn't
even give ear to such a thing.

Dinzie: When the old man here die, Trassie ... when he die, I say,
'twould be the best thing if you moved yourself over into
my father's house, where you'll be safe with your own
people. *(Quickly)* The country is crawling with villains and
lads that do be watching lone women with a thought for
catching them. They'd put you down on a floor in a minute
and go across you.

Trassie: *(Indignantly)* With Neelus in the house, who would bother
me? Neelus will stay as long as I'm here.

Dinzie: *(Mock sadness)* But, sure, you won't be here, Trassie, my
little jewel. Won't you be over sitting down by my father's
hearth and the whole house-full of them bringing you tea
and leaving you in bed in the cold mornings.

Trassie: You'd better be going home now, Dinzie. This is my house
and Neelus' house, and here we'll stay, and we want no one
here but ourselves.

Dinzie: *(As if he had not heard)* You'll be like a queen there with
my father telling you stories and my mother tending to your
every want and Jack here breaking the hasp of his behind to
give you comfort. Tell her, Jack!

Jack: Yerra, Dinzie, I'm no good for explaining.

Dinzie: You don't know the life you'd have. Jack will be up early ...
(Shouts at Jack) Jack!

Jack: That's right.

Dinzie: *(Soft voice)* Jack will be out of his bed with the first light of day to bring in musharoons for your breakfast and when the water be low in the warm weather he'll be capturing white trout for you. We kills four pigs in the one year and think of the puddings and pork steak frying for you and your own cut off every flitch that hangs from the ceiling.

Trassie: If you don't go home and stop your cross talk, I'll call in the dogs out of the yard to scold you.

Dinzie: *(Unperturbed)* I wouldn't like to be you, Trassie, when the old man dies, with no one ...

Trassie: *(Resolute)* I'll have Neelus here with me and I want to hear no more about your house or about your father and mother or about Jack .... *(Jack squirms)* Oh, Jack, you're a man without a mind to let that devil control you. Wouldn't you give a buck jump some day below near Carraig Head and fire him away out into the sea, or wouldn't you find a nice girl and make a marriage bed for yourself?

Jack: The weather'll be getting too warm soon for marriage, Trassie.

Dinzie: *(Calmly)* Don't mind her, Jack! She's only trying to come between us, between two brothers .... two out of the one litter.

Trassie: Wouldn't you go home, Dinzie? Jack, wouldn't you take him up on your back and let my father die in peace. Carry him with you, Jack, out of here!

Dinzie: *(In a rage, strikes the table with his fists)* I won't go out of here! ... I won't go out of here! I have no legs to be travelling the country with. I must have my own place. *(Violent rage)* I do be crying and cursing myself at night in bed because no woman will talk to me. I puts my nails to my flesh *(Grits teeth with temper)* because no girl will ever look at me on account of my dead legs. *(Then indicates his back)* And this impostor here, *(Wrathfully tries to claw the hump on his back)* this hound of the devil, this curse o' God on my back.

Jack: You'll give yourself a fit, Dinzie. We'll go now.

Dinzie: *(Fiercely)* We won't go. My father promised me this place would be mine, and it will be mine. She'll go home to our house. What do she want with a house of her own and land and cattle besides? What do she want with it, when she has no notion of marrying, herself?

Trassie: Close your mouth!

Dinzie: *(Beats upon the table)* I will not close my mouth! *(Opens his mouth pitifully, says sadly)* When I was fourteen years of age I used to be thinking of girls ... thinking I was then and thinking I am now ... and thinking I'll be for the rest of my living days unless I have a house and land to draw women to me.

Trassie: Close up and go! Go now, Dinzie Conlee and leave us alone!

Dinzie: *(Absently)* Will I sing, Jack? I say, Jack, will I sing? *(To Trassie)* I have black teeth, but I have beautiful gums. I can't sing? But I can hum like a honey bee.

Trassie: Are you going to take him, Jack, or will I call in the dogs?

Jack: *(Defensively, weakly)* Sure, if I put him up on my back now he'll kill me with the pucking he'll give me. Wouldn't you be said by him, Trassie, and stay over with us. L'ave him here an' he'll get some oul' woman. 'Twill satisfy him.

Dinzie: Be said by Jack, Trass! Be said by him! Jack is as sound as the tar road you'd be walking on, Jack looks like an ass, Trassie, but he's a pony in his heart. Aren't you, Jack?

Jack: *(Modestly)* Ah, Dinzie!

(Enter Peadar Minogue, from the left)

Peadar: *(Politely salutes the newcomers and addresses Trassie)* How is he now?

Trassie: No sign of a change in him. He's still the way he was.

Dinzie: (*Accusing*) Who's he? Who's he, I say? Who's he, Jack? Threaten him, Jack! Ask him who he is, with his head bare in a strange house. Go on, Jack!

Jack: (*Draws himself up to his full dimensions*) What's your name?

Peadar: My name is Peadar Minogue.

Jack: (*Reflects stupidly for a second*) Why so are you here?

Peadar: I'm a journeyman thatcher.

Dinzie: (*Chuckles*) Could you put a thatch on a baldy head? What call have you to be here? Ask him what call he has to be here, Jack. Go on, Jack.

Jack: What call have you to be here?

Peadar: Searching for work only. I was passing the road by and saw the thatch rotten on this house and I said to myself 'twould be as gay for me to call.

Dinzie: I never heard of the name Minogue in these parts!

Peadar: I'm only going the road looking for work.

Dinzie: The best thing you could do would be to keep on going the road.

Peadar: That's my intention.

Dinzie: Fellows like you upset me, leaving the road, going into houses, looking for bread and meat.

Peadar: I work for what I eat and I always did that same.

Dinzie: You have the look of a man who never had the full of his belly!

Peadar: If 'tis insults you want to cast, cast them! I'm a black stranger here. I mean no harm.

Dinzie: *(Anger)* There was more thrown to dogs in our house than was eat in yours in the round of a year!

Peadar: We were never hungry, and any man that struck the dinner in our house was never hungry.

Dinzie: Who's to say? Every fool will boast about his table. In my house when myself and Jack sit down facing each other there is that mound o' meat and spuds between us that we can't see each other 'atin!

Trassie: *(To Peadar)* Maybe you'd be wanting to wash yourself before you go. You'll find a bucket of water on the small table near the dresser. There's a towel hanging about it.

Peadar: A wash would do no harm.

               (Peadar exits left, looking curiously at the company in the room)

Dinzie: The house will be alive with fleas after him!

Trassie: He doesn't look that way. He's as clean as you.

Dinzie: D'you hear that, Jack. D'you hear the way she's black-guarding your brother?

Jack: *(Half-hearted)* Ah, leave her alone, can't ye.

Dinzie: *(Points finger at sick man in bed)* He won't be long more in the world, Trassie. They're calling him now and he won't go. When he goes you'll be coming over to our house and we'll send Neelus off to the home. *(Trassie makes to protest)* Will you let me talk, Trassie; will you let a poor oul' cripple talk; will you let your own cousin talk? Why do they be all plaguing me, Jack? Trassie, this is the way of it. When your father die, my father will give him a good wake and funeral – won't he, Jack?

Jack: My father said it all right, Trass! He said he'd buy four firkins of porter and a dozen of wine and whiskey and the dearest coffin in the town of Lenamore.

Dinzie:	*(Quickly, as Trassie is about to interrupt)* I will come here then to this place, and I'll find some oul' woman to marry me. *(Pitifully)* Sure, I sees the girls going to chapel every Sunday. They do be lovely with their long hair jumping up and down on their shoulders and their fleshy collops so daintily walking the road. *(Hits the table again)* I must have a girl to marry me.
Jack:	Go aisy, Dinzie, or you'll upset yourself.
Dinzie:	*(Shrieks loudly)* Stop telling me to go aisy! Stop will you, or I'll stick you! 'Tis fine for you that can walk into a dance-hall and catch hold of a woman and dance with her. *(Challenge)* Will you swap backs with me? Will you knock this villain of the Devil's breed from between my shoulders.
Jack:	Your turn will come, Dinzie. 'Twill come in time.
Dinzic:	Don't be teasing. Jack, don't be teasing.

(The old man stirs in the bed)

Trassie:	Wouldn't the two of ye go away home or ye'll wake up my father.
Dinzie:	What does he want waking up for, wouldn't he stay the way he is?
Trassie:	Take Dinzie home, Jack, or your uncle will wake.
Jack:	Come on away, Dinzie. We'll come back again.
Dinzie:	'Come on away, Dinzie'; 'Come home, Dinzie!' Ye're all ag'in me. Have I no feelings at all? Do I see or feel nothing? Which of ye know what I feel ... I watches the lads with their girls over on the strand near Carraig Head in the height of summer. I sees the big mountainy farmers galloping like stud horses through the shallow water and they dragging their girls after them through the spray. Is it how you think I don't notice the way a drop o' water do be shining on the white milky flesh of a young woman?
Jack:	Ah, Dinzie, 'tis only bringing tortures on yourself you are.

Dinzie: I see the handsome young girls and they casting warm looks of longing over the young men and I know what they do be thinking, but none of them cares about giving an eye to Dinzie Conlee. *(Sincerely)* What harm but I would be fonder of a girl than any one of 'em. I would mind her the same as a child and give over to every wish she'd put to me.

Jack: Ah, Dinzie, 'tis only yourself you're hurtin'!

Dinzie: *(Unaware)* I would leave no one say a single word to her in crossness. I would polish and shine her shoes for her like the black of a crow's wing. I would cut her toenails and wash her feet for her in the evening. Oh, I would give in to her no matter what she would say, so long as she would come into my bed at night and hear out the end of my troubles and we could be whispering to each other the small things of the day. *(Shakes fist at the old man in the bed)* Wouldn't you give over, you oul' pizawn, wouldn't you die and have done with it?

(The old man stirs in the bed, rises on an elbow and opens his eyes. Trassie rushes to assist him. The old man, helped by Trassie, sits up in the bed, looks at Dinzie and tries to speak. He stammers at Dinzie who recoils a little. He raises his right hand in threatening attitude towards Dinzie who recoils further. The old man then falls back against Trassie's hands. She lays him on the bed)

Trassie: Will you have no pity for a sick old man? Will you see my father dying and have no consideration for him?

(She lays him gently again on the pillows)

Dinzie: *(Assured that the old man is helpless, lifts his fists towards the bed in fighting attitude and shouts)* Come on! ... Come on, I say! ... Come on, let you! I'm not afraid of you. *(Viciously points his finger at the old man)* We'll beat him, Jack. Did you see him pointing at me, Jack?

Trassie: *(Tearfully)* 'Tis you that should be in the home, not Neelus. Are you taking leave of your senses altogether? My father is dying! Jack, take that brother you have and carry him home to his room and shut him in from all of us.

Dinzie: *(Indignantly)* D'you hear her, Jack? D'you hear what she's saying about your own brother?*(Gently)* Put me up on your back, Jack. Put me up on your back, my own brother.

Jack: *(Hopefully)* Are we going home, Dinzie?

Dinzie: *(Shrieks)* We won't go home! We won't go home! Put me up on your back, Jack. Put me up on your back 'till I attack her.

Jack: The last time you struck a body was at Lenamore Fair and I gave twenty-eight days in jail for you. If you strike Trassic, Dinzie, it might be worse .... *(Menace)* ... If you strike the old man they'll have it that you killed him and 'tis me they'll hang, Dinzie. I'll take no more blame for you. I'd hate to hang from a rope for any man. I won't dangle for you Dinzie. I won't dangle.

(Dinzie thumps the table viciously and scowls)

I didn't mean that, Dinzie, 'pon my soul and conscience, but come on away home. Can't you come on. They'll be wondering what's holding us here all night.

Dinzie: All right, Jack, we'll go! *(Warningly to Trassie)* No more of your nonsense now. I won't have it from you. The minute he's put into his trench I'll be making my way over here. Have your clothes bundled and ready. Put me up, Jack. Put me up and carry me home. *(Jack hoists him on to his back)*

Jack: Have you a grip? Get a good grip.

Dinzie: *(Putting his arms around Jack's neck)* Right, Jack! Right, Jack! Steady, boy! *(To Trassie)* Send word over by Neelus if he takes a turn for the worse.

Trassie: Ye'll have word.

Dinzie: Go on, pony! Go on! *(Clicks his tongue)*

Jack: I told you not to be calling me pony.

Dinzie: Right, Jack! Right, Jack! Right, Boy! *(As if he were* *addressing a pony, clicks his tongue)* Go on! Go on!

(Jack opens the door and exits with Dinzie. Trassie stands perplexed after their departure. As she does so, Peadar enters from the left)

Trassie: Did you eat enough?

Peadar: I had plenty, thanks.

Trassie: Where will you go now?

Peadar: To the west. The men will be busy now with the fishing and there's sure to be work.

Trassie: Have you people of your own anywhere?

Peadar: I have a brother, married, with a small farm in the mountains. I spend the winters there. If I had my bag now, I'd be going.

(Trassie exits and returns with the bag. She places it on the floor)

Trassie: Where will you sleep the night?

Peadar: I'll find a place – maybe a hay shed or an old stable.

Trassie: But how will you sleep without clothes over you? There is cold in the wind, and wet, too, in it from the sea. You would be frozen.

Peadar: I'm well used to it. *(Sincerely)* I was often frozen to the heart, sleeping without shelter.

Trassie: Have you been to the west before?

Peadar: Not as far as this.

Trassie: It is far different from the mountains where you will find shelter. There is no shade here, only the hard wind blowing in to you. It would go through your clothes and sting you.

Peadar: *(Stooping to pick up his bag)* I'll find some place.

Trassie: Wait ... maybe ... maybe you could sleep here if you weren't afraid to sleep with Neelus.

Peadar: Why should I be afraid?

Trassie: Sometimes he goes out and might not come back 'till morning.

Peadar: Where does he go?

Trassie: Down to Carraig Head to have a look at the sea. The full moon and the high tide is the worst time for him or when the peal salmon run in the first days of summer. He acts queerly then.

Peadar: What harm is that?

Trassie: It is not right to be wandering around in the night. *(Then in a tone which has some appeal)* Would you sleep with him and not notice him?

Peadar: I wouldn't notice him. I sleep sound. I would be very thankful for the chance of a bed.

Trassie: You could start away with the first light tomorrow. We rise early here.

Peadar: Do you keep milch cows?

Trassie: We have seven, three calving. We have a few head of sheep. They graze the open mountain that falls into the sea.

(Enter Neelus from the left. He surveys his father)

Neelus: Did they go – Dinzie and Jack?

Trassie: They've gone.

Neelus: Why don't you lock the door on them, Trassie. Lock the door and they can't come in.

Trassie: They're your cousins, Neelus. I couldn't do that.

Neelus: *(Fearfully)* I know what they want to do with me. I hear
them talking. They want to drive me away from here – away
from Carraig Head and the salt water. Where you would see
no seagull against the black of the cliffs. Where you would
never hear the cannon guns in the caves.

Trassie: No! No! No! Neelus ... I won't let them do that! I would
never see you sent away like that. I would never let them
touch my boy – my own dear boy.

Neelus: *(Looking around him fearfully, hands to sides)* I know
Dinzie Conlee. He hates me. He hates you, Trassie. He'll
hunt me away from Carraig Head and the tides. *(Fearfully)* I
won't see the fingers of the silvery tide feeling the goldy
sands before she throws her body down on it. I'll choke and
smother in the black room. They'll hunt you, too, Trassie.
Dinzie Conlee is the Devil!

Trassie: *(Touches his hand consolingly)* We will always stay here,
Neelus ... the two of us.

Neelus: *(Faraway look)* Dinzie and Jack will hunt you, too, Trassie.
(He looks helplessly at Trassie) What will I do, Trassie?

Trassie: *(Looks at Peadar)* He's trying to help me, but his mind is
bothered. *(Neelus nods helplessly)*

Peadar: Why should you want help? Is there something wrong? Can
I do anything to help?

Trassie: No! ... Nothing! *(Hastily)* You mustn't take notice of what
he says. Talk to him for a while. I'll go to fix your bed.

(Trassie looks at her father and exits)

Peadar: What did you mean when you said Dinzie and Jack would
hunt your sister? *(Waits for reply. Receives none)* What did
you mean when you said it? There must be something bad in
store for the two of you. You wouldn't want to see Trassie
hurted, would you? Think, Neelus, of what you were saying
a while back. Think of Trassie.

Neelus: Trassie ... *(Vaguely)* ... Trassie ... *(Gently)* ... Trassie.

Peadar: Yes, Trassie! You wouldn't like if she were hurted, Neelus.

Neelus: *(Awesome)* Below in Sharon's grave where they do be crying ... below in the deep wet black of the cold rocks ...

Peadar: *(Touching Neelus' arm with his hand, says considerately)* No, Neelus! Think! *(Pauses, reflects)* We will follow each other with talk out into the night. I will tell you about the singing finches in Glashnanaon, my country and then, maybe, you'll tell me about yourself and Trassie in your own childish time.

(Curtain)

ACT ONE

Scene II

*The action takes place in the same room as before. The time is the late
evening of two days later.*

The room is changed – in as much as there are now several chairs in it.

*On the bed the old man lies dead. He is facing the audience slightly
propped up. He is dressed in a brown habit. The bed is made neatly
underneath him. The uppermost clothes are white.*

*Brass candlesticks, holding lighted candles, stand on a table. There is
also a saucer filled with snuff, on the table.*

*A prayer-book props the old man's head up. A rosary beads is entwined
in his hands.*

*Neelus – dressed in a new suit of coarse quality, stiff collar and new
brown boots – stands near the closed door, hands behind his back. He walks
towards the bed, looks at the old man, and turns again to the door, standing
impatiently, hands behind his back. He continually screws up his face and
admires his new clothes with his hands.*

*There is a subdued knock at the door. Neelus is alert immediately. He
lifts the latch and stands aside.*

*Enter two women, one tall and one small. The tall one is a cadaverous,
sad-looking person; the other short and stout and of a nosy disposition –
both in their middle fifties. They are followed by an old man, Tom Shaun.*

*The tall woman is Moll, the small woman Mague. Both shake hands
with Neelus sympathetically. Tom Shaun shakes the hand of Neelus and lays
another on his shoulder. Tom Shaun is aided by a walking stick.*

Mague:	What time did he die, the poor man?
Neelus:	Last night late.
Mague:	Had he a lot of pain?
Neelus:	No! No pain! He only left a little gasp out of him.
Mague:	*(To Moll)* Wasn't he lucky to have no pain?
Moll:	He was blessed.
Mague:	*(To Neelus)* Did he say anything an' he dyin'?

Neelus: He did! He said, 'God take me out of my misery!'

            (Both women sigh sympathetically)

Mague: Any more?

Neelus: He said we'd get rain in the course of a few days ... I have
            his watch. *(Takes silver watch from his pocket and fondles
            it)* Trassie gave it to me. It loses three minutes in the day.

            *(The women shake their heads sorrowfully and advance to
            the bed)*

Moll: Ah! God bless him, isn't he a handsome corpse!

Mague: He's lovely, the fine decent man.

Moll: That had a hard word for no one.

Mague: That would give you the bite he'd be eatin'.

            *(Moll feels the quality of the cloth of the habit and says to
            Mague)*

Moll: The best of material.

            *(Both take pinches of snuff, apply it to their noses, and
            survey the room)*

Moll: *(To Neelus)* Where's Trassie?

Neelus: She's feeding the men in the kitchen.

Moll: Is there many of them there?

Mague: Did your cousins from Luascawn come?

Moll: What about your mother's people from Lenamore?

            *(Neelus does not reply but goes forward and holds the watch
            to the ears of the women, and Tom Shaun)*

Neelus: D'you hear the little heart thumping inside?

(Neelus returns to the door. The two women exchange meaningful glances. Both kneel, bless themselves and commence to pray. They then take their places alongside two other women already seated from the beginning of the scene. All four women pay out their beads through their fingers and whisper decades of the rosary to themselves. Neelus holds the watch to his ear, smiling. A knock at the door, Neelus lifts the latch and stands aside. Two more old women enter and follow the procedure of Moll and Mague. When all six women are seated they take up a low and mournful keening which Neelus is fascinated with. Enter Trassie with Peadar, the latter bearing a tray of filled tea cups which Trassie distributes to the old women. Peadar remains at a distance and is joined by Neelus. When the opportunity presents itself the women keen and lament)

Neelus: They're all looking at you, Peadar, wondering who you are and where you came from.

(Tom Shaun lights his pipe)

(Peadar turns and looks calmly at the women)

That's Peadar Minogue, the thatcher. He sleeps in the one bed with me. *(Proudly)* He hails from Glashnanaon where the singing birds do be. He tells me all about the singing birds before we go to sleep.

Woman 1:   You're welcome to these parts, Sir.

Peadar: Thank you kindly.

Tom Shaun: Would you, by any chance, be anything to the Minogues of Tooreentubber that used to keep the boar?

Peadar: I have heard tell of them but there's no relationship between us.

Tom Shaun: The Minogue bonhams were as hardy as terriers. There was a piebald in every litter.

Peadar: No, there's no relation.

Tom Shaun:	There was a Minogue, now, a small block of a man, a thatcher, too, by the same token – Thomas Timmy Minogue they used to call him. He married into six cows in Glounsharoon. He used travel to Aonachmore pattern in a common car. A jinnet he had and the white knight we used to call him. That same jinnet was a born gentleman. *(Having divested herself of this, Woman 2 lights a pipe. The formal atmosphere relaxes as the women quiz Peadar)*
Peadar:	I heard tell of him, too, but we're not connected.
Woman 1:	*(Brightly)* What would your mother's name be now? Is she alive or dead?
Peadar:	She's dead this long time, the Lord ha' mercy on her. From Errimore, a Hennessy.
Tom Shaun:	*(Reflectively)* Hennessys from Errimore, Hennessys from Errimore. Hennessys. There was a Timmineen Hennessy, a flamin' stepdancer, from the Errimore side. Would they be the one Hennessys?
Peadar:	Timmineen Hennessy was my grand-uncle.
Tom Shaun:	Glory be to us all, but isn't it a small world. *(Looks around for proof)* and you tell me Timmineen Hennessy was your grand-uncle? Sure, his feet were like forks of lightning. He would dance on a three-penny bit for you. Have you any step yourself?
Peadar:	I can dance a hornpipe.
Tom Shaun:	Kind for you to be able! Kind for you ! *(Reflectively in wonder)* And Timmineen Hennessy to be your grand-uncle. Was there ever better than that?
	(Trassie takes tray and goes towards the exit. She turns)
Trassie:	*(To Neelus)* Will you come to the kitchen and have something to eat?
Neelus:	I want to stay here at the door.

Trassie: You can eat later on. *(To Peadar)* Will I bring you something to drink?

Peadar: Thank you ... but I have no mind for it.

Trassie: You must be tired – up all night, with no sleep.

Peadar: Glad to give a hand only.

Trassie: Maybe you would like to go out in the air. It would put new life into you.

Peadar: I'll walk a little ways, so.

(Peadar goes towards the door where Neelus is, watched closely by the seated women. Neelus opens the door for him. Exit Peadar. Trassie exits left)

Moll: *(To Mague)* There was a Banshee heard calling over the inches last night.

Mague: Notice in plenty.

Tom Shaun: *(Who up to this has not spoken)* There was an ould bard of a tomcat with whiskers like needles by him, crying over the inches last night.

Moll: *(To Mague):* The Banshee gave three long cries of torment every while.

Tom Shaun: *(To no one in particular)* This ould whiskery tomcat used to leave three lonesome cries out of him every while.

Moll: *(Angrily)* For a finish there was one long terrible cry and then no more.

Tom Shaun: For a wind up didn't this ould cat leave one long terrible cry out of him, that you would hear in the other world. Calling, he was, for his little pussy and she never came to him. You'd swear it was the Banshee that was crying but it was only an oul' whiskery tomcat.

(Moll gives the woman a withering look)

People do be easily fooled. I'm goin' to the kitchen for a drop of the hot stuff. *(He exits. Tom Shaun returns at once with whiskey)*

(The women now keen unrestrainedly, tear their hair and comfort themselves)

(There is a knock at the door. Neelus lifts the latch and stands aside. Enter a well-dressed woman in her forties. She walks as if she owned the world. Her accent is precise. She shakes hands with Neelus and kneels by the bed in prayer. She is the local schoolmistress, Miss Dee. There is respectful silence while she prays, broken only by Neelus who takes a pinch of snuff. Miss Dee rises and sits on a chair near the main door and alongside Woman 1)

Miss Dee: Good evening, everybody!

Moll & Mague: *(Ingratiatingly)* Good evening, Miss Dee.

Miss Dee: *(To Tom Shaun)* Must you smoke when a man is dead? *(Tom Shaun quickly puts the pipe away. Neelus comes forward and holds the watch to Miss Dee's ear. She strikes his hand violently. Frightened, Neelus returns to the door)*

Miss Dee: *(To Neelus)* Where is Trassie?

(Neelus hangs his head)

(Firmly) Don't try to fool me, boy. I know what goes on in your head. You're not half as simple as people think. Where is your sister? *(Neelus points a finger towards the kitchen)* Do you mean she's in the kitchen? *(Neelus nods)* And why don't you say so? Making signs as if you were dumb.

Woman 1:   *(Meekly)* And how are all your scholars, Miss Dee?

Miss Dee: They are not my scholars, my good woman. I merely teach them.

(The women nod in agreement)

Miss Dee: *(Turns to Moll and Mague)* What in heaven's name are you nodding at? If you have something to say, say it. I fancy if that poor man on his death-bed could say something, he would, and be very glad if he could.

Neelus: I know who's coming now! *(Puts his ear to the door)* I know who's coming now!

Miss Dee: Whatever are you talking about?

Neelus: My cousins, Jack and Dinzie.

Miss Dee: *(A little anxiously)* How do you know?

Neelus: Because I know the heavy fall of Jack's feet from carrying Dinzie.

(Suddenly there is a loud knocking at the door. Neelus stands well back. The latch lifts and the door opens)

Dinzie: *(From without)* Go on, Jack, boy! Go on, pony!

(Enter Jack, carrying Dinzie on his back. Jack shakes hands with Neelus. Neelus puts the watch to Jack's ear, then to Dinzie's. Dinzie snatches the watch and puts it into his own pocket. Neelus stands cowed, hands covering his head)

Go on over to the bed Jack. Go on.

(Jack carries Dinzie to the bed)

Bend over him 'till we see is he dead.

(Jack leans forward. Dinzie touches the corpse lightly)

(To corpse) Are you dead, Donal? Are you dead, I say? Look at the face of him, Jack. Are you dead, Donal, I say? Will you have me talking to myself? Is he dead, Jack?

Jack: *(Placatingly)* Oh, wisha, Dinzie, he's dead all right. Leave him alone and don't be tormenting him.

Dinzie: Go on Jack. Go around 'till we see who's here.

(Jack takes Dinzie around)

Dinzie: *(To Moll and Mague)* What business have ye here? A nice pair of old hags, snuffin' an' gossipin' an' drinkin' yeer little sups of tay an' cuttin' an' backbitin' everybody.

(Jack carries him to where Miss Dee sits)

Dinzie: Who left you in?

Miss Dee: I came to pay my respects to the dead.

Dinzie: You came spyin' to see who was here. Why don't you get an oul' man for yourself an' get married?

Miss Dee: How dare you!

Dinzie: *(Mimicking her voice)* How dare you! How dare you!

Miss Dee: You should be on your knees, praying for your dead uncle.

Dinzie: Should I, now?

Miss Dee: Yes, you should, and show a little respect for the dead.

Dinzie: *(In a rage)* Give her a lick of a fist, Jack.

Jack: Ah, can't you go aisy, Dinzie! Isn't it a wake-room we're in!

Dinzie: Go on, give her a lick! She used to give me slaps at school long ago when I usen't know my tables. She used to give a poor oul' cripple slaps. *(Pretends to cry most unholy, lunatic wailing and weeping)*

Miss Dee: *(Viciously)* You richly deserved every slap you got. You were the wickedest boy in the school. I didn't slap you half enough.

Dinzie: Oh, good God, Jack, are you going to let her talk to a poor defenceless cripple like that? Ketch her by the throat, Jack, and give her a squeeze.

Jack: But sure you well know I can't, Dinzie. We'd have the law on top of us. I went to jail before for you, Dinzie. I know what 'tis like.

Dinzie: Only for a month! Only for a month, Jack. And wasn't it worth it?

Jack: Are you going to sit down at all?

Dinzie: You're mad to be rid of me. *(Shouts at Neelus)* Who's below in the kitchen?

Neelus: *(Fearfully)* A crowd of men drinkin' and 'ating.

Dinzie: *(To Jack)* Come on down and we'll rise a row with some-one.

Jack: *(Pleads)* Ah, can't you stop. Isn't it a wake-night? Wait until we're going home.

Dinzie: Frightful scampin' coming to examine a dead man and spillin' porter all over the house. A wake house is worse than a public house. We'll ketch some fellow half drunk and we'll give him a most unmerciful pucking goin' home.

Jack: Will you sit down now for a while? My back is achin' with the pain.

Dinzie: Put me down, Jack boy. Put me down, let you.

Jack: Where will you sit, Dinzie?

Dinzie: Put me down there Jack, where I can keep an eye on all of 'em.

(Jack places Dinzie on a chair where he commands a view of all. Jack goes through the motions of exercising his cramped muscles. Dinzie pulls his legs up under him in the chair. Jack goes through his exercises on the floor. The keening begins anew, more restrained. Dinzie listens piously for awhile and raises a hand)

Dinzie: *(Surveying crowd)* The quarest lookin' bart of weeds I ever witnessed. Wouldn't ye go away for yeerselves and not be annoying the poor man in the bed.

Miss Dee: You'll answer for your sins yet.

Dinzie: What do you want me to do? Start screeching and roaring with sorrow an' pull the hair out of my head in lumps.

Miss Dee: You are to be pitied! Can't you at least keep silent in the presence of death?

(This only serves to goad Dinzie on)

Dinzie: Jack, are you listening? I say, are you listening, Jack?

Jack: I am, Dinzie.

Dinzie: Do you know what I'm going to do when I die, Jack? Will I tell you?

Jack: *(Resignedly)* Go on, Dinzie! Tell me!

Dinzie: Well, Jack, when I be stretched out dead in my bed with a brown shirt on me like the lad here and my face the colour of limestone, I'll send the orders beforehand to Coolnaleen townland for Nell Keown, the concertina player, and I'll get about fourteen fiddlers from all over the parish and I'll have all of 'em playin' at my wake. I'll have porter to swim in and whiskey in tanks and I'll poison half the parish with drink. *(Laughs)* That'll be the sport, Jack, I'll have geese, Jack – roast geese, and male and rolled oats for this gang here. *(Points to Miss Dee)* We'll get a ladder for her and put her sittin' on top of it where she can see all. *(To Miss Dee)* Will you come? Ah, you will! Ah, you will! You'll come all right. Sure, there'd be no sport at all without you. *(Plucky, violently mischievous)* Ah, do, say you'll come. Say you'll come. 'Twould be no good being dead if your puss wasn't facing me. *(Changed tone)* I swear I'd wake up and give a roar at you and carry you screechin' to the coffin with me.

Miss Dee: If it wasn't for the respect I have for the dead, I'd leave here this instant minute.

Dinzie: Do you know what you must do, Jack, when I'm dead? You

> must pull a thick ashplant and put it beside me in the coffin and when they're shoulderin' me to the church yard, Jack, I'll hit the cover of the coffin a kick and knock it off ...

Jack: Ah, stop, Dinzie!

Dinzie: And sit up inside o' my coffin and flake the four polls of the livin' bastards that's carrying me to my grave.

Miss Dee: The curse of God attend you!

Dinzie: I told you, Jack, you should have given her a kick. *(Threat to Miss Dee)* Would you give me a slap now for not knowing my tables? One and one is two. Two and two is two. Three and two is two. Two and one is nine. Come on, give me a slap! *(Slowly)* If you give me a slap now, I'd hang for you, woman!

(Enter Trassie)

Dinzie: Will you be ready to go after the funeral tomorrow?

Trassie: Will you take something, Jack ... a drop o' whiskey?

Jack: I'll chance it.

Dinzie: Don't give me the deaf ear, Trassie, I won't take it from you. By God! I won't. You can be ready to go tomorrow evening.

Trassie: *(Notices Miss Dee)* Oh, Miss Dee! I didn't see you. Will I bring you something?

Dinzie: Bring her a fist of oats and a gábhail of hay. She's braying there with hunger since she landed.

Trassie: A drop o' wine?

Miss Dee: Just a little drop, if you please. *(Trassie exits)*

Dinzie: *(Loudly, boastfully)* I'll have my heels up on the hob of this hearth tomorrow night and maybe a woman of my own after a while. Jack, you'll be the best man at my wedding. I'll be well catered for. I'll have good times presently. I say, Jack, I'll have good times.

Jack: You're fond of yourself, Dinzie.

Dinzie: *(Wonder)* Fond of myself! I like myself Jack – every man likes himself, Jack, hump or no hump. I knew a fellow once going with a girl and he was fond of himself. *(Pauses reflectively)* He was so fond of himself that every time he'd give her a rub, usen't he to give himself a rub too.

Miss Dee: *(To Moll)* How's your husband keeping, these times?

Moll: *(Delighted to be asked)* Oh, he's fine, thank you.

Miss Dee: *(To Mague)* And you, Mrs Hallissey! How's your son in America?

Mague: Oh, he's going great entirely. He sends home ten dollars every week.

Miss Dee: Isn't he a good boy to do that?

Mague: *(Proudly)* Every week of his life he sends it. I get my envelope every single Monday morning from Jotty King, the postboy, with the ten dollars pasted inside and he sends a great bundle of money at Christmas, too.

Dinzie: *(Triumphantly, to nobody in particular)* Isn't that more of it an' they'd be bla-guardin' me for wanting a wife. Sure, isn't it well known that the postboy wasn't near her door in the space of five years since the shop-keepers got tired of sending her bills for the meal and flour she owes. *(Smiling to the ceiling)* God help us! They do be boasting about their sons and about the money they get. *(Tone of impeachment – to Mague)* Wouldn't you tell the truth. 'He sends you home ten dollars every week!' He sends you home nothing! Ye spend yeer days slaving for yeer sons and go into debt to send them to America. And what do they do when they land in America? Forget about ye. And aren't they right, too? Isn't it a blessing in itself to get away from ye.

Miss Dee: Have you no consideration for the feelings of other people?

Dinzie:	Give us a song, Jack! Go on, Jack, give us a song – a lonesome one.
	(Enter Trassie with drinks on a tray. She hands same to Jack and Miss Dee. Jack swallows his in one gulp. Miss Dee sips genteely)
Trassie:	A biscuit, Miss Dee?
Miss Dee:	No, thank you, Trassie. I don't care for sweet things.
Dinzie:	Are you going to ask me to have anything? Is it how you think I have no mouth. Firing drink into black strangers and leaving your own flesh and blood go dry!
Trassie:	You know what happens to you when you take drink?
Dinzie:	Nothing happens to me ... nothing ... nothing. Ye're all down on me.
Trassie:	You're welcome to what we have in the house, but drink only sets you stone mad altogether.
	(Exit Trassie)
Dinzie:	*(To Neelus)* Come over here!
	(Neelus advances timidly)
	(Taking watch from pocket) Do you want your watch back?
Neelus:	*(Nods fervently)* I do! ... I do! ...
Dinzie:	Right you are, so! ... down with you to the kitchen and the first bottle of whiskey you clap your eyes on, put it under your coat and bring it up to me. Mind you let no one catch you, or I'll dance on top of your watch.
	(Neelus hurries to the kitchen)
Moll:	*(Rises)* 'Tis time we were going home, Mague, girl.
Dinzie:	What's your hurry? Yerra, sit down a while and rest your-

self. Sure, aren't you going all day. Go on, sit down a while.

(Doubtfully Moll sits, Neelus hurries in and produces a partly-filled bottle of whiskey, triumphantly, from under his coat. He hands it to Dinzie and extends his hand for his watch. Dinzie shakes hands with him and drinks with relish from the bottle)

Cock-a-doodle-doo!

(He swallows lengthily again, puts the bottle on the ground and rubs his hands together with delight. He motions to Neelus as if he would whisper with him. He whispers something into his ear. Neelus nods understanding and hurries out by the front door)

Jack:	What did you put him up to now, Dinzie?
Dinzie:	*(Drinking from bottle)* Cock-a-doodle-doo! ... Cock-a-doodle-doo! ...
Jack:	Ah, what did you tell him to do, Dinzie?
Dinzie:	Soon enough we'll know, Jack.
Jack:	Ah, can't you tell us, Dinzie?
Dinzie:	'Twill make a good year for hay ... I say, 'twill make a good year for hay, Jack.
Miss Dee:	I hope you haven't put that poor boy up to any mischief.
Dinzie:	Out for a gallop I sent him, to loosen him out.
Jack:	Ah, Dinzie, you're a fright, you are!
Miss Dee:	If you put that poor simple boy up to anything bad, God will visit you for it.
Dinzie:	We'll have the kettle on for him when he comes!

(All the women assume shocked expressions, sighs of hor-

ror, etc.)

Dinzie: *(Drinks from the bottle again)* Cock-a-doodle-doo! ... Cock-a-doodle-doo ... doo ... dooo ... *(Shrieks of laughter)*

(Enter Neelus by the front door. He goes immediately to Dinzie. He has something under his coat. First he extends his hand to Dinzie for the watch. Dinzie hands him the watch and Neelus takes a leather whip from under his coat and hands it to Dinzie. Dinzie accepts it and puts the bottle aside)

Jack: What's that for, Dinzie?

Dinzie: Not for you, Jack! Did I ever use a whip on you, Jack?

Jack: No, but you often threatened me!

Dinzie: Yerra, wasn't I only coddin' you. Put me up on your back, Jack, like a good boy.

Jack: Sure you won't flake me with the whip?

Dinzie: No fear, Jack. Is it me whip my own little pony? Come on now, Jack. Give us a hoist up.

(Reluctantly, wearily, Jack puts Dinzie up on his back. Dinzie cracks his whip)

Dinzie: D'you know what we'll have now, Jack. We'll have tables.

Jack: Tables, Dinzie?

Dinzie: Tables is right, Jack. Two and two is four. Tables, Jack. *(Contemplates)* We'll start with Miss Dee. *(To Miss Dee)* How much is the cost of seventeen quarts of porter, if blackberries were a guinea a bundle?

(Miss Dee frowns irritably)

(Clicking his tongue) Should be four slaps by right, Jack, but we'll try her with another one. Hmmm! Let me see now ... how much is the price of nine canisters of nettles if hearts is

trumps an' the ace is robbin'?

Miss Dee: Get away, you cheeky bla'guard!

Dinzie: She's very bad, Jack, very bad! Four slaps I'd say now!

Jack: Ah, can't you stop, Dinzie? If you don't be quiet now I'll put you down again.

Dinzie: *(Menace)* If you do, I'll choke you.

Jack: Ah, sure, I was only mockin', Dinzie.

Dinzie: I'll give her one more question and if she doesn't answer it I'll have to give her the slaps. Fair is fair, Jack. We can't have no favourites. Now, the last question. Supposin' you left water flowing into a bucket when would you have it filled? ... *(Waits for answer)* ... Ah, Jack, there's no meaning to this ...

(Dinzie suddenly leans sideways and gives Miss Dee a smack of the whip across the ankles. Miss Dee jumps up with a scream)

Miss Dee: Oh, you little hellion! I'll have the law on you! ...

(Miss Dee retreats backwards towards the kitchen)

Dinzie: After her, Jack! ... After her! ... After her, the wine-sucking gossiper!

(Dinzie makes several attempts to whip Miss Dee secondly but she runs into the kitchen. Dinzie guides Jack back triumphantly and confronts Moll and Mague)

Dinzie: Two lively scholars, here, Jack!

Jack: Ah, Dinzie, 'tisn't right. There'll be trouble. What will happen if Miss Dee goes for the guards?

Dinzie: She'd be afraid to go for the guards. Doesn't she know what'd befall her after. We won't be in jail for ever, Jack! Now, we'll test out the lassies here. *(He draws the whip*

downwards at the six women on the chairs) Go on, ye
thievin' hussies, gallivantin' around the country, spyin' on
people an' back-lashin' and cutting.

*(Dinzie whips the women into the kitchen. Neelus bolts out
through the front door in terror. With the room empty,
Dinzie raises the whip aloft)*

Glory, Dinzie Conlee! Glory to the man who hunted the
grabbers and snappers. Glory to his brother Jack who carried
him up on his back. Glory to the bould Dinzie for a
gaiscíoch and a hayro and may scabs and scour descend on
all the vagabonds and villains that come to people's wakes
to gossip and spy like beggars for whiskey and porter, for
snuff and tobacco.

Jack: Ah, go aisy, Dinzie. Go aisy, let you!

(Dinzie gives Jack a vicious wallop in the back)

Jaminy, but you'll capsize me, Dinzie! You've hurted me,
man!

Dinzie: Put me down Jack. Put me down 'till I get a rest after that.
We cleared the room, Jack – Dinzie Conlee and his brother
Jack. *(Jack puts Dinzie on the chair. Dinzie lifts the bottle
and hands it to Jack)* Drink up, Jack. 'Tis great for the
gizzard!

*(Jack swallows heartily from the bottle and shakes his head
after it. Jack might roll on floor and kick out like a horse,
whinnying as he does)*

Jack: 'Tis strong stuff!

Dinzie: Give us a song, Jack!

Jack: Ah, I wouldn't like to, Dinzie.

Dinzie: Glory to Jack Conlee, with the voice of a thrush.

Jack: *(Doubtfully)* Would it be any harm, do you think?

Dinzie: No harm at all. Won't it shorten the road for him? *(Indicates the corpse)*

Jack: Will I give 'The boys of Ned's mountain'? 'Tis an airy one.

               (Jack assumes a singing stance and clears his throat. Enter Trassie. She glares at Dinzie)

Trassie: Are you going out of your mind ... what right have you to drive all these people out of the room? Whipping Miss Dee and the women the same as if they were cattle. How dare you do that in this house where you have no right.

Dinzie: No right! ... Isn't this my house now?

Trassie: It is not your house!

Dinzie: *(Shrilly, thumping the chair)* 'Tis my house! 'Tis my house! You'll be comin' over to our house when we bury what's in the bed.

Trassie: I'm going down to the kitchen to tell the people you're sorry – that you didn't know what you were doing, you were so foolish with the drink.

Dinzie: Tell them nothing, or I'll use the whip again. I'll mark 'em this time. I swear I'll mark 'em. I'll file the skin off their bones.

Trassie: *(Menace)* Dinzie Conlee, I'm going down into the kitchen now, and I'll be coming back to this room again in the space of a few minutes. If you aren't gone home, I'll call the dogs in from the yard.

Dinzie: Don't be upsetting me now! Don't be upsetting me. I have a plan in my head.

Trassie: A plan! ... What plan?

Dinzie: We'll have Neelus examined.

Trassie: Examined! ... By whom?

Dinzie: By the father of all doctors.

Trassie: He was examined before by doctors and they said there was nothing to be done. They said he was harmless.

Dinzie: *(Thumps the chair)* He isn't harmless, I tell you. Wait 'till he be examined by a proper doctor and we'll soon find out what's wrong with him.

Trassie: What are you talking about?

Dinzie: *(Pause)* Pats Bo Bwee!

Trassie: *(Wonder)* Pats Bo Bwee!

Dinzie: Pats Bo Bwee, the Cures, from the Wiry Glen. He has cures for all aches and pains, for every dizaze you could put a name to.

Trassie: He's not a doctor!

Dinzie: He's better than any doctor.

Trassie: He's a quack!

Dinzie: D'you hear that, Jack? D'you hear her? D'you hear what she is calling Pats Bo Bwee? A man that could read your mind for you? She's calling Pats Bo Bwee a quack? If he heard you he'd turn the eyes around in your head, and give you a dose of the itch.

Trassie: Maybe he has cures, but he's not a doctor.

Dinzie: He'd lose what doctors are in the country. There was an old man, blind, beyond Lenamore, that never saw the sight of day or night in twenty years. Pats Bo Bwee gave him a black bottle and a clatter into the side of the poll with his brass hammer and didn't the sight come back to him and he saw twice as much as he saw before.

Trassie: He knows nothing about Neelus.

Dinzie: What harm what harm, 'tis how you're afraid to bring him over. 'Tis how you're afraid of what he'll tell you, for you know well in your heart and soul that Neelus is as cracked as the crows and worse he's getting.

Trassie: I am not afraid. Why should I be afraid?

Dinzie: Pats Bo Bwee will put his finger on the harm. You know he will and you don't want Neelus' trouble to be known.

Trassie: I know what Neelus' trouble is.

Dinzie: Ah ... but *do* you know what his trouble is? If you're so sure why won't you let him be examined?

Trassie: I'm not afraid to have Pats Bo Bwee see him. Why would I when I know that Neelus is as harmless as a child in the crib?

Dinzie: I'll have Pats Bo Bwee here the day after the funeral. I'll tell him to bring his brass hammer and his bag of cures. Thanking me you should be that I'm doing this for Neelus. Wait 'till Pats Bo Bwee is finished with him and you'll soon know what the trouble is ... Put me up on your back, Jack, and carry me home ... carry me home, Jack!

Jack: *(Helping Dinzie on to his back)* Get a good grip, Dinzie. *(Hoists him on his back)*

Dinzie: Don't be giving out wine and whiskey to them scroungers in the kitchen. That's all they're here for, for what they can get out of you. *(To Jack)* Go on, pony ... go on up, there. *(Hits Jack on the back)*

Jack: Didn't I tell you not to be calling me 'pony'. Do you want the people of Baltavinn to be calling me 'pony'.

Dinzie: Yerra, 'tisn't a pony you are at all, Jack, but a horse. Sure, you're desperate strong. Open the door and we'll be going ... I'll have Pats Bo Bwee over the day after tomorrow ... go on, Jack! Go on – are you going to keep me here all night?

(Jack opens the door and exits, with Dinzie on his back. When they have gone, Trassie tidies the room and collects a

few discarded empty glasses from the floor. After a few moments the latch lifts and Peadar Minogue enters)

Trassie: Did you go a long ways on your walk?

Peadar: Just over the fields a piece, down to where there is the deep hole with the sea coming in under it – the hole they call Sharon's grave.

Trassie: That is a dangerous place! Many is the fine cow that fell into it, never again to be seen. You know the story?

Peadar: But that is a pagan story, surely, and not one you could believe.

Trassie: Oh, to be sure, it is a pagan story but the old people ... many of them believe it to be true.

Peadar: It was sad that Sharon should die in such a way.

Trassie: It is lonesome to think of her falling into the dark and sad to think of her young sweetheart waiting, never again to see her.

Peadar: Thinking about it would be lonesome.

Trassie: Sometimes when the moon is a full moon over the sea, Neelus will go down and sing lullabies for Sharon, thinking to give her sleep.

Peadar: No harm in it, surely, that he should want to help a soul in trouble.

Trassie: I shouldn't be talking like this with my father dead. Praying I should be!

Peadar: A thing to talk about is good. I saw your cousins from the fields. I could see the small fellow, on his brother's back. Like a horse and jockey they were. The two of them were singing to wake the country. *(Hesitantly)* Was there any trouble while I was out?

Trassie: Nothing to bother about.

Peadar: If there was trouble, I could help, maybe!

Trassie: *(Looks at him as if she would tell, but changes her mind. They look at each other)* How could you help and you next to nothing to me and it would be no way fair to expect you to interfere. People like you are kind but relatives are the very devil and a death in the house makes them ten times worse and turns life into a bedlam.

(Curtain)

ACT TWO

Scene I

The action takes place in the kitchen of Trassie Conlee's farmhouse. The time is four days later, mid morning. Trassie is cutting seed potatoes at the table. She wears a sack over her skirt. She uses a common kitchen knife for the cutting. While she is thus occupied Peadar Minogue enters by the front door.

Trassie: What is the day doing?

Peadar: The day is holding up fine. There's a dry wind from the sea and there's no rain likely.

Trassie: Did you see Neelus?

Peadar: I saw him. He had the drills opened for the potatoes. He was starting to draw manure.

Trassie: 'Twould be an ease to get the potatoes down. We could begin with the bog then. We have three sleens of turf to cut and make up. I suppose you'll be going your road now?

Peadar: 'Tis time to go, I'd say! I am very thankful to you for keeping me these last days.

Trassie: 'Tis how I should be thanking you ... the great help you were to us.

Peadar: That was nothing.

Trassie: Will you go back to your brother's house now, or will you go north in search of work?

Peadar: I think I'll chance the north – the Kerry Head direction – cross over into Clare. There should be work.

Trassie: What kind is your own home in the mountains?

Peadar: Only a small place with the grass of a few cows.

Trassie: Is your brother the older of the two of you?

Peadar: No, I'm a year older. My mother died after he was born.

Trassie: God rest her! ... Shouldn't the place be yours, though, if you are the eldest?

Peadar: It was willed to me by my father.

Trassie: And how is it, then, that your brother has it?

Peadar: He married a girl he was fond of and he had no place to take her, so I gave the place over to him.

Trassie: And did you not think to marry yourself?

Peadar: I thought about it often enough but there was no one I was fond of.

Trassie: *(Pause)* Wasn't it foolish to give away your house and land and cattle?

Peadar: There is always a place for me there. My brother is a good brother and his wife is a kindly person.

Trassie: Would you think of working at anything else besides the thatching?

Peadar: I am best at the thatching, but I wouldn't turn away from a day's work of any kind.

Trassie: There is work here for a few weeks, maybe longer, if you like to stay. We would pay what we could.

Peadar: There is no need for payment. I would be very happy to work here for my keep.

Trassie: Why is that?

Peadar: *(Awkwardly)* It is a nice place to be.

Trassie: There will be hard work in the bog, and then there are the crops and the corn.

Peadar: No matter! I'll get used to it.

Trassie: What do they call the place you come from?

Peadar: Glashnanaon.

Trassie: That's a nice name – Glashnanaon!

Peadar: 'The stream of the birds'!

Trassie: I know! Are there many birds there, then?

Peadar: It is a great place for linnets. And you could hardly count
the swarms of finches. 'Tis the first place you'll hear the
cuckoo and come the winter the pilibíns fill the sky with
their call so that, all in all, winter or summer, we have our
fair share of birdsong.

Trassie: All you will hear in these parts is the seagull or maybe the
curlew crying in the rain when 'tis dark and stormy. The
curlew crying is lonely but it is nice to hear when you have
a good bed to sleep in.

Peadar: Maybe you will come visiting some time to my brother's
house in Glashnanaon. You could bring Neelus. He would
like to see the finches.

Trassie: Maybe some day when the weather is fine we would go
visiting. It is nice, too, here in Carraig Head in the height of
summer. You can sit on the trippols of finnaun over the cliff
and you would see the ships passing down the coast, little
ships only.

Peadar: I imagine it would be nice of a fine day to sit and watch the
ships passing. I hope there will be work enough to keep me
through the summer. It would be nice.

Trassie: Maybe there will. We have three mountain meadows that
have to be cut with a scythe. Plenty work in that. 'Tis settled
then that you'll stay for a tamaill?

Peadar: If you want me.

Trassie:	It would be good to have you. There is money to be made in the pooleens of the stream that flows near the meadows. A man with a good net and a head on his shoulders wouldn't want for salmon. They fetch a fair price in Lenamore in the summer.
Peadar:	It wouldn't be my first time poaching salmon. Of course, a man alone ... *(shrugs)*
Trassie:	Neelus is afraid of the pooleens but I have an eye for bailiffs as good as any man when the salmon are there.

(There is a knock at the door, a long steady knock)

Who could that be, at this early hour of the day?

Peadar:	Maybe Dinzie Conlee and his brother.
Trassie:	They would never knock.
Peadar:	Who, then?
Trassie:	Maybe a tinker man looking for the colouring of his tea or a stranger enquiring his way. You would never know at this time of day. *(She moves towards the door and calls)* Who is it that's out?
Voice:	*(Thunderous, yet refined, of most musical south-western tone)* Pats Bo Bwee with his bag on his back. Pats Bo Bwee, from the Wiry Glen.
Trassie:	*(Excitedly)* Pats Bo Bwee! Oh! Dia Linn! Looking for Neelus he is.
Peadar:	I heard tell of Pats Bo Bwee. That's the man with the great name out of him for cures.

(Trassie, flustered, opens the door. Enter Pats Bo Bwee. He is sixtyish, florid, bearded, with a great advance-guard of a stomach. He carries his leonine head thrown back. He wears a small coat tightly buttoned over his protuberance of stomach. He carries a bag on his back. He wears an ancient hat with a large quivering feather. He wears corduroy

trousers, hob-nailed boots and shirt open at the neck. He gives the impression of health and vigour belying his years. He surveys the kitchen indulgently)

Pats: The last time I put my foot inside this door was twenty-seven years ago. Kawtee Conlee, your grandmother, was alive at the time. She was suffering from 'the runs'. It nearly killed her, but I cured her. 'Tis four walking miles from the Wiry Glen to Baltavinn and four more back.

Trassie: *(Arranges a chair for him)* Will you sit down, and I will make tea for you? *(Anxiously)*

Pats: It was a great sorrow with me that I wasn't here for your father's wake. I was beyond in Glounsharoon attending to the father of nine children. He got a swelling on his elbow and I gave the best part of a week curing him. By all accounts it was a wake to be remembered! I drinks tea but seldom. There is great boasting in Baltavinn about the whiskey that was brought to this house. A man was heard to say that 'twould take a week to drink it.

Trassie: There's whiskey left if you care for it. I should have asked you in the first place. You'll think very poorly of us in Baltavinn, the small respect we show you ... I won't be long.

(Exit Trassie. Pats Bo Bwee goes and sits on the chair previously proffered by Trassie. He places his bag between his legs and his stick across his knee)

Pats: What name have they for you?

Peadar: My name is Peadar Minogue.

Pats: What keeps you here?

Peadar: There was a death ...

Pats: What is death but a long rest beyond the door and no more! What is death but a slipping away till we gather again.

(Peadar makes no answer but walks a little to and fro)

(Authoritatively, pompous) You say your name is Peadar Minogue. I say my name is Pats Bo Bwee. I am Pats Bo Bwee with my one yalla cow and my cures. But who are you?

Peadar: I'm Peadar Minogue, the thatcher.

Pats: *(Stamps foot)* But what keeps you here?

Peadar: I stay here only for Trassie Conlee.

Pats: And you tell me you stay here only for Trassie Conlee! Do you ever get pains?

Peadar: No pain yet. I thank God for that.

Pats: Where is the boy of the house?

Peadar: There are no boys here, or girls either – only two men and the one woman.

Pats: I'm cursed with the flowers of genius. I'm danged from thinking nether thoughts. I'm wore, wore to the bone thatcher. Now where is Neelus Conlee that's gone simple?

Peadar: Neelus Conlee is out working his day's work.

Pats: When is he due to arrive?

Peadar: For his dinner.

Pats: Is there meat for the dinner?

Peadar: I couldn't tell you that. I'm not boiling it.

Pats: You'll be eating it.

Peadar: What's boiled must be eat.

Pats: What's boiled must be eat indeed. Otherwise why boil! *(Winningly, to Peadar)* What time is dinner?

Peadar: It changes, day in, day out. Noon one day. Evening the next.

One should wait for the call.

Pats: Did you travel, thatcher?

Peadar: Some!

Pats: Ah, but did you travel the mind? ... We were all at Aonachmore at the pattern and there's more went to America, but did you travel the mind ... strange roads in that country, thatcher!

(Enter Trassie, with two glasses in her hand, one filled with whiskey and the other partly filled. She hands the small quantity to Peadar and the large one to Pats Bo Bwee, who accepts the large as his due)

(Toasts) God increase wakes. *(Taking a goodly swallow of whiskey – toasts)* That we may never lose the tooth for it! *(Swallows his drink in a gulp)*

Trassie: *(Taking glass)* Would you have more of it?

Pats: Enough is enough! We mustn't make pigs of ourselves. 'Twould be as well to bring in the boy of the house. I have a call to make in Goildarrig to a stutterin' child and I have a woman calling to the Wiry Glen tonight with blisters on her behind. There's a heifer calf in Trieneragh with the white scour – all waiting to be cured.

Trassie: Was it Dinzie Conlee told you to call?

Pats: *(Surprised only slightly)* He told me that young Neelus Conlee was ailing with a troubled head. It should be aisy to cure for there is no dúchas. I never heard of a Conlee being soft in the head.

Trassie: There is nothing much the matter with Neelus. There were two doctors from Lenamore with him and they said he would always be the same. They said he would never be violent but that he was finished with words of sense.

Pats: *(Uplifts his head)* Doctors must account for their aisy lives. They always have some story for you. Mind you, I don't condemn. We must be on the one word. You'll never hear of a thrush eating another thrush.

Trassie: Peadar, will you call Neelus in from the fields.

Peadar: *(Putting his glass on the table)* I'll call him in.

Pats: *(Uplifts his head)* I'll call out and call him in! *(Rises pompously. Points at the bag)* The curse of the crows on the hands that interfere with the work of Pats Bo Bwee or goes near his bag.

Trassie: What harm would it do if some one else called him?

Pats: Did you not ever hear of the devils in hell? The way they do have their ears cocked? Do ye know the misfortune that might befall your brother if one of ye called him? There's no devils at all in hell except a few tending their fires. The rest of 'em, to be around tormentin' people and coaxin' them and working their best plans to fool them. *(Dramatic pause)* God forbid that Pats Bo Bwee would ever say a word against the devils. We all have our faults and 'tis as well to be in with the two sides. 'Tis only a brave man like myself that would open his mouth against either of the two, with the grave staring me in the face.

Trassie: Let you call him yourself, so. Far be it from me to go putting obstacles in your way.

(Pats Bo Bwee goes to the front door, opens it and looks out, standing with great dignity – stomach protruding)

Pats: Let ye put no hands to my bag or be for feeling it to find what's inside fearin' ye might come to harm.

(Exit Pats Bo Bwee. After he has gone Trassie resumes her seed-cutting, slowly, abstractly. Peadar walks nearer to her)

Peadar: Trassie!

Trassie: *(Startled)* What is it?

Peadar: Do you think that this Pats Bo Bwee or what's in his bag will cure a person or ease a troubled person? What I mean is that Neelus is what he is, 'tis delicate, the handling. A man should want to know him well.

Trassie: There is a great name out of him for curing.

Peadar: It could be – but who is to cure a troubled mind?

Trassie: There is no harm in attempting it. I know, as well as I know my own hands, that Neelus is harmless.

Peadar: Why so do you allow Pats Bo Bwee to examine him? Why should you let a man like that decide what thing is before your brother?

Trassie: Because I know there is nothing up with Neelus.

Peadar: *(Deliberate tone)* I will be leaving Baltavinn tomorrow or the day after.

Trassie: I thought to hear you say you would be staying a while.

Peadar: I don't hold with what's going on! I don't hold with Bo Bwee or your cousins Dinzie and Jack Conlee.

Trassie: I am doing the best thing I know.

Peadar: There is nothing in the oul' bag except maybe bottles of water or cut rushes.

Trassie: They say he has great powers and by all accounts there's a bad curse out of him.

Peadar: If he is so wise why is it he is the way he is? Why should he be so full of draoidheacht and mystery instead of saying his say openly. An honest man will give you his whole mind.

Trassie: *(Hurriedly)* You never gave your whole mind. How is one to know what's in a person's mind, anyway?

Peadar: How do you mean?

Trassie: How do I mean, only that you were a stranger first and now I don't know what you are for sure.

Peadar: *(Embarrassed, puzzled)* Just that I was a bit bothered about ye.

Trassie: Why should you be bothered about Neelus or about the cures of Pats Bo Bwee? *(Hurriedly)* Why should you be troubled about the way things are in this house or why should you trouble yourself to stay at all when you are so well used to the roads? Or what private thing of your own keeps you under the one roof so long? *(She cuts the seed quickly)*

Peadar: I stay here ... *(Looks away)* ... I stay here because you were pleasant and not full of pride when I first put my foot inside your door.

Trassie: Was that what brought you then, the chance of a bed with sheets, and the chance of keeping your feet under a table three times a day with no worry of the roads before you?

Peadar: I was hungry often and many a night without a bed but many a man without a home to go to will find himself in the same tangle of trouble. It's nothing to a single man who has no one to worry about him.

Trassie: You have a free life. Fine for you to be so.

Peadar: I travelled every road of the west coast but I never gave more than two nights under a roof in the same house. The urge not to remain was in me. I have given the best part of a week here, what I have never done.

Trassie: *(Charmingly)* Why *do* you give so much time here?

Peadar: *(Pause)* You!

             (Peadar turns to examine the wall at the rear. Trassie stands stock-still)

Trassie: It's time I looked after the dinner.

Peadar: It's early yet.

             (Trassie is about to return to the table to continue to cut the

potatoes)

Peadar: *(Throatily)* There is a pile of things I could tell you, if you let me.

Trassie: What things?

Peadar: *(Turning, uncertain tone)* I would say you are among the best girls I have seen upon my rounds.

Trassie: Go on with you!

Peadar: I would say things all day to you.

Trassie: *(Without rising her head)* What things?

Peadar: I would say that you have eyes in your head like a stormy evening; that you have calves to your legs like a pair of running trout; that you have a voice that would keep a man awake at night thinking, and, above all things, that you would be a lovely person to have near-abouts to be telling things to. I would say I would like to have soft hold of your two hands.

Trassie: You would say that.

Peadar: I would say that. I would say likewise that I would love to sit and watch you at your work. I would love to see you moving here and there and be watching and admiring you. I would think things then to myself about you.

Trassie: What things?

Peadar: Things, maybe, you would not like.

Trassie: Only a miser would keep a nice thought.

Peadar: If you want to hear, so here it is. *(Bends head)* I would think of the beauty of you, of the way your eyes do be, and how I would give my heart and soul to be lying down in your bed and to be holding you and feeling your softness against me. It is too sweet and hurtful to think of it. To think of the lovely body under your clothes, and to think of the wintry

nights when I would be shielding the soft trembling white-
ness of you from the cold and we whispering together in a
room with nobody else in it.

Trassie: You should not say that!

Peadar: I am a man, amn't I? ... You are a girl of rare niceness with
pretty ways to you and a neat form by you. If I said another
thing I would be telling lies. I have a terrible longing for
you, growing worse lately, growing worse every time you
will look my way.

Trassie: It is wrong of you to be saying this with my father only
barely buried.

Peadar: *(Angrily)* The dead are dead and won't they be always dead.
Will you have them rise up again out of their graves and be
changing the pattern of things that are alive and with us.
(Gently) I'm sorry, Trassie, to give you hurt. I know the
feelings you store for your dead father and I am weak for
your sorrow. *(Dramatic pause – Peadar is in real anger –
violent anger)* But I swear by the Lord God that made me, I
will have the life of Dinzie Conlee if he comes here again
before I leave; if he comes here again frightening you. I've
seen the look of worry and fear in your eyes when they're
here. *(Angrily)* I will let no man frighten you!

Trassie: 'Tis temper now!

Peadar: *(Calmly, slowly)* Temper is what it is! What else would I
have except it was temper. I will! ... I will! And I swear this
by the mother of God ... I will tear the heart out of Jack
Conlee, your cousin, if he lays a hand on you. *(Uplifts his
finger)* I will! ... I warn you! ... I will take the life blood
from the two of them if they make a fool of your brother
Neelus. It was not my place here to interfere but there is too
much of thievery going on and I will not sing dumb when I
see it.

Trassie: I never thought to see such a temper in you! You're like a
devil with temper.

Peadar: *(With humour)* I'm worse than a devil. I'm a man.

Trassie: *(Gently, seriously)* I would not like to tease you, Peadar.

(Peadar goes and takes Trassie's hands suddenly in his, holding them roughly)

Peadar: Now I have your hands and, God forgive me for a coward, I haven't the courage to see what's in your eyes.

(He lets go of her hands and looks directly at her. Trassie closes her eyes, Peadar places his hands over them and he takes her face in his hands. She opens her eyes, and smiles at him)

Now I have your head in my hands and your lovely face under my fingers, and I have to feel you ... I have to feel you for the ease of my body and my mind. I have to feel your kind back within my hands and your lively breasts to my chest. I have to feel the ease of the woman that you are against me. *(She yields wholly to his embrace)* I have to hold you against me for I keep the picture of what is happening now with me. It is joy to hold you, Trassie – pure joy!

Trassie: *(Whispers)* Peadar!

(Peadar holds her tightly and kisses her face and, finally, her lips. The door opens and Neelus enters. He looks stupidly at Trassie and Peadar, who break apart. Trassie resumes her work and Peadar stands to one side. Neelus is followed by Pats Bo Bwee)

Pats: M'anam an diabhail, but this is a great wall of an idiot. Four times I called him and four times he hung his head. 'Come up here, you gamalóg!' says I for a finish, but there wasn't a hum or a haw out of him, so I caught him by the sleeve of his coat and brought him here. Does he be like this always?

Trassie: There is no harm in him.

Pats: Doesn't he know I have people to cure in other parts. You will have to give me the use of the table there.

(Trassie gathers the potatoes into a pot. Peadar turns to watch. Pats Bo Bwee takes his bag and with ceremony

places it on the table. He directs Neelus to sit on a chair.
Neelus sits in a frightened way)

Trassie: This is Pats Bo Bwee from the Wiry Glen, Neelus. He is
only trying to help you.

Pats: He has the wild eyes of his grandfather.

Peadar: What will you do for him?

Pats: *(To the ceiling – pompously)* Ye will all leave the kitchen
now, a-barring myself and the boy. Too many times rogues
and scoundrels have stolen my cures and made fortunes for
themselves.

Peadar: What would I want with your oul' cures?

Pats: Every spailpín in the country is aching for the knowledge I
contain, and when they can't have it they will have curses
pouring down on the top of me ... *(Magnanimously)* What
harm, if it will make them content. I bear no hate ...
(Distantly, slightly reproving) Ye will leave now! I have
work before me. This is no place for common people.

(Trassie takes Peadar by the hand and leads him through
the side exit. He follows grudgingly)

Pats: Hide nothing from me, gearrcach. I have seen the minds of
people like you before. The priest hearing sin in his box will
forgive what he's told, but Pats Bo Bwee will find out
hidden things.

(Pats opens his bag delicately and produces a hammer with
a head of brass. The head is highly burnished, the handle
delicate and of tiny circumference. Pats lays the hammer on
the table and explores further into the bag. He produces
several stalks of mature rag-wort and lays them on the
table. He produces a number of egg-shells, cup-shape as if
the shells were neatly divided (these would be for measures
of medicines). He lays several of these on the table together
with a handled clay container, gallon size, which he shakes
and holds to his ear. Satisfied, he places the container on
the table and takes his brass hammer in hand. He passes in

*front of Neelus and takes his stand at his side. He holds the
hammer behind his back and surveys Neelus professionally)*

Pats: Is it women that's troubling you, or is it the stars? *(Neelus
looks frightened)* I think a tip of the hammer is what you
want.

*(Ceremoniously he brings the hammer to the front, fondles it
and suddenly taps Neelus on the head, with some force. He
leans forward eagerly)*

Did you feel that? Did you feel as if someone spoke to you?
(Neelus looks at him) Out with it!

Neelus: *(Hesitant)* I remember to hear my father talking when I was
small.

Pats: Aaah! ... you did, did you! So well you might, you mad
scut! So well you might, what more?

Neelus: *(With some ray of understanding)* I remember the bed, with
my mother, and to see my father shaving and to be watching
him. *(Neelus pauses, dejectedly)*, and to be playing with
Trassie in the meadows *(Absently, lovingly)*. And Trassie
taking me by the hand to school and I remember Trassie
with her white dress at confirmation. Trassie was sweet.

Pats: Go on! Go on, you folbo! Tell!

*(Enter Peadar angrily with Trassie clutching his hand.
Peadar pauses and he hears Neelus)*

Neelus: *(Rubs his head)* I remember my father ... to sit in his lap ...
(Wanderingly, truthfully) To sit on his lap and be warm,
secure, like the pony in the stable ... and to watch him
smoking his pipe and he looking at me, laughing. They were
all outside my father's lap. They were all outside. I saw the
entire lot looking in at me and they watching my father ...
my father ... *(Loneliness, abject)* ... my father and he lifting
me up into the air ... the strength of my father ...
(Pathetically) ... Dada! Dada!

(Pats taps Neelus viciously with the hammer)

Pats: Dada! Dada! Is your head that empty? When your father was buried you were laughing and talking to yourself or so the countryside says. Is your memory as short or is it going altogether?

Neelus: *(Childishly – to impress Pats. Tone of awe)* The rain is belting the black rocks and the white horses are rearing in the sea. Sharon is olagóning in her grave and Shíofra is screeching in the belly of the wind.

Pats: *(Stands back in amazement)* Oh, Lord God in your fine house above us with angels and saints attending to you, give me patience with this fool – who is seven different kinds of a fool. Come away from your angels and saints and give ear to the words of Pats Bo Bwee and tell me not to tamper with the mind of this bollav.

Peadar: Leave Neelus alone!

Pats: He is to be examined, and he will be examined. No man interferes with Pats Bo Bwee.

Trassie: *(Fearfully)* It might be better to leave him alone, Peadar.

Pats: *(To Neelus)* We will go up to the room and bolt the door and I will work my cures in peace.

Peadar: *(Snatches the hammer from Pat's hand)* You will work your cures without this.

Pats: *(Draws himself to his full height)* I will work my cures with nothing at all. *(To Neelus)* Up to the room!

                 (Neelus rises and goes to the room quietly, followed by Pats Bo Bwee who turns and looks at Peadar)

                 Minogue, from the bogholes of Glashnanaon, put my hammer from you or your hand will waste. They say that Glashnanaon is a hive of thieves. They say that if a man stuck out his tongue there 'twould be stolen off him by the thieving tricksters of Glashnanaon.

                 (Pats Bo Bwee turns and exits the room after Neelus.

Peadar throws the hammer on to the table in disgust)

Peadar: Trassie, there is no meaning to having that man in the house. You know as well as I do that he is as false as a boghole. You know well that he was sent here by Dinzie Conlee and that he was paid money by Dinzie Conlee to come here.

Trassie: Everyone sends for Pats Bo Bwee when all fruit fails.

Peadar: Are you so much afraid of Dinzie Conlee, Trassie?

Trassie: Dinzie is dangerous! Jack is bad but you could fight with Jack and you could beat him but you couldn't beat Dinzie. Not Dinzie. Nobody could get the better of Dinzie Conlee.

Peadar: I see nothing to fear in either of the pair of them.

Trassie: You don't know Dinzie, Peadar. Dinzie would do for you. Do you know he carries a long knife with him in hide where no one can see it? He can be sweet, too. He'd let on to be all about you and that's the time you couldn't trust him at all.

Peadar: I wouldn't fear him. I'd watch him.

Trassie: No! No! Leave Dinzie alone! He's madder than anything in this world. He has no faith in anything. You couldn't trick with Dinzie. He might be doing one thing but he would still be watching all things. You'll never know what he's watching or what he's thinking.

(Enter Pats Bo Bwee, triumphant – pushing a dejected Neelus in front of him)

Pats: *(In a rage – throws his hands. To Neelus)* There's a devil in you! Clear out, you devil you! The devil is 'ating away at your mind and sould and you're clear and clane mad altogether. There is no cure for you that grows in the ground. God give me a silver bed in heaven for the patience I have with you.

(Frightened, Neelus flies before Pats' fury. Pats stands in the doorway calling)

Go on! Gallop away like the mountainy jackass that you are. Gallop away from the sight and sound of God-fearing people. Gallop away into the wind and the wild air where demons are dwelling and sweeping around the bare windy roads of the sky! ... Go! ... Go!

Trassie: Is something wrong? What's wrong with him? Where is he going? *(Innocently)* Did you send him on a journey?

(Dignified, Pats returns his cures to his bag, takes his stick in hand and slings his bag over his shoulder. He stands up with great hauteur)

Pats: I will cure warts, boils and carbuncles. I will put hair growing on a man's palm. I'll put a woman by way of having a child and I'll knit broken bones *(Loudly)*, but I vow! I vow to you, that I will have no truck with geowckacks.

Trassie: Geowckacks!

Pats: Geowckacks and fostooks like that savage of a brother you have, that would take my sacred life but for that he was afraid of my brassy hammer.

Peadar: Your brassy hammer is on the table!

(Pats quickly accepts the hammer and conceals same on his person)

Pats: Where is he, you say? ... *(Points stick at door)* Where is he but gone as fast as his legs will take him to the gravelly slopes of the moon.

Trassie: But why ... ?

Pats: *(Pointing his stick upwards)* Because he's mad! ... Mad! ... Mad! *(He opens door)* He's as mad as a flea on a hot coal. I'll have no handling of him. He's as mad as the heidle fo peeb and the heidle fo peeb is as mad as the breeze. Dinzie Conlee instructed me well. Dinzie Conlee said he was mad all along. I should have taken the advice of sensible people and stayed away from this house where a common thatcher is the master. *(Exit Pats Bo Bwee with dignity, closing the door behind him – Trassie stands a moment and then resumes her preparation for the dinner but then withdraws dejectedly from the table and sits on the chair nearest her and buries her face in her hands and is seen to be crying – Peadar stands idly, helplessly, watching her)*

(Curtain)

ACT TWO

Scene II

The action takes place in the kitchen as before. The time is a day later. It is evening.

Trassie sits near the window, patching the sleeve of an old coat. While she is thus engaged Neelus enters. He sits on a chair near the table, clasping and unclasping his hands, despondently.

Trassie peers at him carefully.

Trassie: Where is Peadar?

Neelus: You does be kissing with him and he does be holding you. *(Trassie holds her breath)* There is a storm outside, Trassie, I see the two of ye holding together the day of Pats Bo Bwee.

Trassie: *(Nervously)* You did not!

Neelus: I see him with his hands around you, givin' kisses on to you.

Trassie: What harm is there in kissing or holding?

Neelus: *(Tearfully)* I have no girl. I have only Sharon below in her grave and she crying the whole time and Shíofra do be scolding her.

Trassie: That is only an old bit of gossip for ageing people. Why do you be going down there at night like an old fool, singing to them, leaving your warm bed behind you? ... The day we take the calves to town, I will buy you a Jew's harp.

Neelus: And ... a red concertina with a yellow belly?

Trassie: I will buy that same.

Neelus: And a fiddle and a German flute for me too?

Trassie: A fiddle and a German flute for sure and certain, the day we sell the calves.

Neelus: *(Somewhat appeased)* What else will you buy for me?

Trassie: *(Motherly tone)* Oh, I will buy you an aghaidh-fidil for the Wren's day at the year end. *(Stops sewing and looks upwards)* I will buy you a gansey coloured yellow and green with white cuffs and I will buy you books with pictures of ships in them and black shiny shoes with buckles on.

Neelus: *(Childish, serious)* Did Sharon wear black, shiny shoes, Trassie?

Trassie: *(Reproach, mild)* Sharon is part of your head, Neelus!

Neelus: What else will you buy for me?

Trassie: *(Dreamily)* Oh ... I will buy currant-tops that you like and a white collar for your stripey shirt and maybe a hat for you going to Mass and maybe togs for bathing, and we could go down to the tide, Peadar and myself and yourself.

Neelus: *(Shakes his head in wonder)* Did Sharon have a hat on her head, Trassie? *(Looks up dreamily)* Or was it a ribbon she wore or a comb to gather the length of her golden hair. What was it she wore, Trass?

Trassie: Who's to know what she wore, Neelus, since 'tis years since she was drowned. Sure, nobody would take notice of Shíofra or Sharon or how is one to know they were there at all?

Neelus: *(Mysteriously, confidentially)* They were there all right, Trass. I does often hear them when you does all be in bed. *(Wonder and fright mingled)* Well, if you hear poor lovely little Sharon and she is giving sighs and sobs to the wind and her tears to the tide *(Then hatefully)* and that other little thing, that Shíofra, is never done with screeching back at the wind, out of temper, Trassie.

Trassie: *(Resumes her stitching)* You were very good, Neelus at our poor dada's funeral ... *(Pauses)* ... the mud on his boots and the sigh of him when he bended to take them off – my father. *(Sighs)* The stories he used to tell us. *(Smiles sadly)* The gay stories about cats that wore waistcoats and bonhams that wouldn't eat their dinner unless they were dressed in collars and ties and the crows that used to go to their own schools the same as ours.

Neelus: *(Clasping and unclasping hands)* Poor dada ... poor dada ... every small bird I see on a tree or hopping, I think to myself of my poor dead dada.

(Enter Peadar Minogue)

Peadar: There's a desperate storm rising on all sides. 'Twill make a wild night. I wouldn't wish to be in a boat on the sea tonight.

Trassie: The clouds were flying across the sky all day – always the sign of a storm.

Neelus: Wait until you hear the wind tonight!

Peadar: Awful screeching like the inside of a pig's bladder if you blew it up and left it off. The Goureen Roe was calling for the rain in the bog.

Trassie: What about the sheep?

Peadar: I counted them all near the house. They're safe enough. They know the storm is breaking. Sheep aren't as foolish as people think.

Trassie: *(Putting the coat aside – rises)* Will we have a game of cards to pass the long evening?

Peadar: 'Twould give us something to do. What games do ye play in Baltavinn?

Trassie: 'Beggar thy neighbour' or 'A hundred and ten'. I'll get the deck in the room.

(Exit Trassie)

Neelus: I see you with your hands around Trassie.

Peadar: I am very fond of her.

Neelus: Why are you fond of her?

Peadar: I don't know why.

Neelus: Is she fond of you?

Peadar: I hope so, Neelus. I think, maybe. She might be a little bit fond of me. I hope she is.

Neelus: *(Mournfully)* I have no one that's fond of me!

Peadar: Trassie is fond of you, man; and I'm fond of you.

Neelus: Dinzie Conlee isn't fond of me!

             (Enter Trassie with a pack of cards)

Trassie: We will play 'a hundred and ten'. Neelus can deal.

             (They draw chairs to the table. Neelus sits at the head, Trassie at centre and Peadar at the bottom. Neelus deals three hands of five cards each and five to the side. They examine their cards)

Neelus: We will play for pennies. I'll chance twenty.

Trassie: I pass!

Peadar: I'll pass too

             (Neelus takes the five other cards quickly and examines them and throws them down again)

Trassie: 'Tis hard to beat Neelus at 'a hundred and ten'. He has a great brain for following cards.

             (Neelus deals cards secondly to Trassie and Peadar, but drops the cards halfway through and sits bolt upright)

Trassie: What's wrong, Neelus?

             (Neelus does not answer but sits listening. Trassie looks at Peadar)

Peadar: What's wrong, Neelus?

Neelus: It's them!

Peadar: Them! Who?

Neelus: 'Tis Dinzie and Jack, I hear Jack's feet.

Trassie: Oh, merciful God! And we having such peace.

(The three sit silently watching the door. Jack and Dinzie can be heard to approach. The door opens and Jack enters carrying Dinzie on his back)

Jack: Will I put you down, Dinzie?

Dinzie: *(Thumps Jack into back)* Aren't you in a great hurry with the poor oul' cripple. Set back a bit, let you, 'till we see what's here. Go back, pony ... back, boy ... back! *(Dinzie forces Jack to retreat while he surveys the occupants of the kitchen)* D'you see them, Jack? ... Ah, Jack, will you have a look at the faces of the craturs. Wouldn't you love to be like them? *(Loudly – pompously)* There should be no gambling allowed where there was death! 'Tis flying in the face of God. 'Tis the end of the world when people show no respect for the dead. Ye should be ashamed of yeer lives – gambling and arguing and cursing over money with yeer father roasting below in the halls of hell. Ye'll have no luck for it.

Jack: Will I put you down, Dinzie?

Dinzie: Will you go aisy! You're like an oul' woman, grumbling.

Jack: *(Wearily, first trace of anger)* Amn't I after galloping to the Wiry Glen today to see Pats Bo Bwee, and in to the town of Lenamore to Macky Flynn, the motor, and amn't I after coming here on top of it. You give me no peace or ease.

Dinzie: *(To trio)* Do you know at all what I'm going to do to Jack? I'm going to buy a pony's harness with bells on it for him and a reins made out of light leather and I'll make silver shoes for his feet.

(Dinzie gives Jack a thump in the small of the back. Jack winces and sets Dinzie down on a chair. Jack goes to the corner and begins to limber up and exercise his cramped muscles. He does this exaggeratedly. Then he takes off his coat and cap and helps Dinzie off with his. He goes through his exercises on floor)

Dinzie: *(Perched on the chair)* Ye'll be ready in the morning, Trassie.

(All watch him)

Trassie: Ready for what?

Dinzie: *(Vicious)* Ready to put your feet under you and leave here!

Trassie: Are you mad?

Dinzie: Not mad but in earnest! Today, myself and Jack walked all the ways to the town of Lenamore. We were telling the civic guards about Neelus and they said 'twould be safer to have him locked away.

Trassie: *(Rises)* What lies did you tell the civic guards?

Dinzie: I told what was true.

Trassie: You told lies, I know.

(Peadar rises and glowers at Dinzie)

Peadar: Better to take no notice of him Trassie.

(Dinzie fumes and thumps his chair)

Dinzie: *(Hysterically)* Listen to the lying tramp of a thatcher. Put me up on your back, Jack, 'till we kick the stomach out of him. Put me up, Jack, and we'll dance on his guts.

(Jack goes to Dinzie's side. Peadar advances a step, fists clenched)

Trassie: *(Command)* Peadar! *(Peadar stops)* Go out, to the stall and see if the cows are all right, and pacify the pony. He's afraid of storms.

(Peadar looks at her doubtfully, and looks at Dinzie again, clenching his fists)

Peadar: What about him?

Trassie: Go out now, Peadar, I'll be all right. I'll call if I want you.

(Peadar exits casting threatening looks at Jack and Dinzie)

Dinzie: That's right! Take the side of wandering villains that would murder you in your sleep.

(Dinzie scowls at Neelus. Neelus rises, looks fearfully at Dinzie, and exits)

Trassie: Why do you be always putting the heart crossways in Neelus when he has never done anything to you?

Dinzie: Because he's a blasted nuisance that should be under lock and key. We were at the Wiry Glen this morning, myself and Jack. Isn't that right, Jack?

Jack: That's right, Dinzie.

Dinzie: We were talking to Pats Bo Bwee and he's not feeling well, the poor man, after his visit to this house. He swore on his oath that Neelus will smother us all some night in our sleep. He swore on his oath that there's no madder amadán of a man from here to Donegal. Isn't that right, Jack?

Jack: He said it, all right, Trassie.

Trassie: And how much money did you give him?

Dinzie: *(Mystified)* Money! What money? Give him money for what? Explain to me, Jack, what she's saying. I never gave him money. That I might be as dead as my auntie Noney that's in her grave and my uncle Pat that was slaughtered by the turkeys in Salonika if I gave him money. Money for what?

Trassie:	How much did you pay Pats Bo Bwee for saying Neelus was dangerous?
Dinzie:	*(Puzzled)* What ails her, Jack, what ails her now? Sure she don't know what she's saying at all, Jack. God forgive her, she's getting wilent. 'Tis that rat's spawn of a thatcher that has this house upset. A man told me in a public house in Lenamore that you couldn't be up to the Minogues – that they were the greatest tribe of pratey-snapping mongrels from Goilldearg to the salt water.
Trassie:	Go home, Dinzie. Take him home, Jack. He has no business here.
Dinzie:	*(Thumps chair)* That's the respect she has for her uncle's son, her own flesh and blood, that's for her good.
Trassie:	*(Firmly)* Dinzie Conlee, you're going out of this house now and you'll never come inside the door of it again. Take him up, Jack, and carry him away.
Dinzie:	*(Thumps the chair, shouts)* I will not leave here! I will never leave here! My place is here! I want a little woman of my own to marry here! No one will have me if I haven't a house and land. What would you do if you had this millstone of mine on your back? What would you do if you had only dead branches of legs? What would you do if you were never to feel the grassy ground under your feet or never to vault a gate or a ditch and you passing through land? What would you do when the fiddles are tuning up for the sets and everyone tapping toes on the stone floor? What would you do when the lads are kicking ball and you have a wild feeling to draw a kick for devilment? What would you do?
Trassie:	'Tis hard for you, I know, but it is no fault of mine. Go away from here – home!
Dinzie:	*(Bitterly)* Aisy for you and for Jack here with yeer legs firm and strong and yeer straight backs. *(Shrieks)* I have nothing at all to show for myself. I have twists and turns to my body like a thorn tree. *(Roars)* I'm no fool! Dinzie Conlee's no fool. I know my value but if I have this place I will have plenty single women thinking of settling with me. *(Plead-*

ing) Will you condemn me for that, Trassie? ... For thinking the way I do? *(Pause)* Everybody knows you yourself would have no trouble latching a man to you and I swear to God I will give you what few pounds I have to add to your fortune if you let me have this house. *(Pause)* ... And a bit o' land ... *(Pause)* ... and the few cows ... and the pony. *(Placatingly)* Won't we go visiting Neelus in his fine tall home when we get the fine day ... and the roads dry?

Trassie: *(Sincerely)* 'Tis a pity for you, but ... I have doubts about you – the way you made plans for Neelus as if he was mad.

Dinzie: *(Reverting to old, demoniacal self)* He is mad, I tell you! He's stone mad!

Trassie: How do you know but maybe 'tis yourself that's mad?

Dinzie: *(Thumps chair)* In what way would I be mad when I'm as sane as a man of ninety? Sure, you never heard anyone saying that I was mad.

Trassie: They be afraid to say it – afraid of yourself and Jack.

Dinzie: D'you hear that, Jack? Good almighty God, Jack, I say, did you hear that? I say, Jack, that's the last of all!

Trassie: You have some spatter of sense, Jack; take him away with you now.

Jack: Ah, faith, I will not take him away. 'Twould be a great aise to me to see him settled here. Sure, hasn't he my back nearly broken. Sure, aren't there hollows in my shoulders from his hands and my ribs are black and blue from the pucking he gives me. I'm a pure martyr from him.

Dinzie: Hush, Jack! Hush, pony!

Jack: Don't be calling me 'pony', Dinzie! The young lads going the road to school does be saying 'Hup!' to me now and ... *(Clicks his tongue several times)*, 'Go on there, horsey!' 'Tis not fair, Dinzie.

Dinzie: Ah, sure, don't I only be coddin' you, Jack. Sure I wouldn't say a word to my own little pony. Sure, wouldn't I lick the ground under your feet, man dear, I'm so fond of you.

Jack: You have a quare way of showing it.

Dinzie: Be ready in the morning now, Trassie. Be ready with your coats and dresses and hats, and we will have the motor here in the daytime for Neelus. 'Twill be a happy day for him.

Trassie: *(In real anger)* Get out of here, you demon!

Dinzie: *(Loudly)* I won't go home! I won't! There's nothing at home for me, God help us! Nothing but an empty bed and a corner out of the way. I'll be master here, with my own woman pampering me.

Trassie: I'll bring the gun down out of the room to you.

Dinzie: Bring what you like. Nothing will move me out of this seat. My place is here!

Trassie: I will call Peadar.

Dinzie: *(Shocked)* Oooh ... Ooooooh! ... You will call Peadar! Did you ever see a paper bag blown up, full of wind. *(Puffs out his cheeks to show, then claps his hands violently)* Jack will crack in his head like that and send his brains squirting all over the ceiling. *(Draws a large clasp knife from his pocket and displays the blade)* I'll rip him open with this, the same as you'd open a sheep's belly. Bring her over to me, Jack. Bring her over and when she'll be done with me, I promise you she'll be anxious to do what I say.

Jack: Ah, Dinzie, poor oul' Trassie is only a girl. Sure she'll go all right. Say you'll go, Trassie. Tell him you'll go an' be quiet then. There's no knowing what plan he'll think of if you don't give in to him.

Trassie: I will not give in to him. Why should I? This is my place and Neelus' place and nobody, not even Dinzie Conlee, will ever put us away from what's our own.

Dinzie: *(Loudly)* Ketch her, Jack, and bring her over to me.

Jack:	Ah, Dinzie, don't ask me!
Trassie:	*(Nervously)* Pay no heed to him, Jack. Don't be said by him, Jack. He'll get you in jail again, and this time they won't leave you out in a hurry.
Dinzie:	*(Slowly, throatily, tightening his grip upon the knife)* Ketch her, Jack, and bring her over to me, 'till I get a grip on her.
Jack:	*(Afraid)* Ah, Dinzie ...
Dinzie:	*(Slowly)* 'Don't mind Dinzie,' she says. 'Don't mind your own brother.' *(Hopelessly, in a wonderfully plausible vein)* O holy, holy saints, Jack, she's putting mountains between us, boy. 'Tis a terrible sight to see a person coming between two borned brothers or does she know what she's saying at all, Jack? Does she know the trouble our mother had rearing us?
Trassie:	*(Determinedly)* Stop your prattle. Stop trying to work Jack's will and all our wills and clear away out of here.
Dinzie:	*(Sincerely)* For the last time, Jack, I'll ask you to ketch her by the hair of the head and bring her over to where I am.
Jack:	You don't mean it, Dinzie!
Dinzie:	*(Fiercely)* I'll lob this knife between the breasts of her and stick her like a pig if you don't ketch her, Jack. You'll see the blade of this buried in her, and the handle standing out from her bosom like a paling stake in the depth of a hollow.
Jack:	*(Turns directly towards Trassie)* I'll have to ketch you, Trassie ... *(Trassie eludes him)* Stand aisy, Trassie!
Dinzie:	Blast you, you oul' fool, make a drive at her and pull her hither.
Jack:	*(Confident)* I'll ketch her!
	(Jack makes another advance towards Trassie but again she eludes him and succeeds in opening the door and calling loudly)

Trassie: Neelus! ... Neelus! *(Then quickly)* Peadar! ... Peadar!

(As Jack advances towards the door she suddenly avoids him by availing of the table and they watch each other dartingly)

Dinzie: *(Excited)* Jump over the table at her and you have her.

(Jack outstretches both hands as if he were herding geese and tries to get Trassie into a corner)

Jack: Cush! Cush!

(Jack warily advances at one side of the table. Trassie immediately avails of the other side)

Dinzie: Pull the table out of your way and you have her.

(Jack lifts the table and drops it suddenly to face Peadar Minogue who has entered quickly, through the open door)

Dinzie: *(Yelling)* Aha, the thatcher is landed. Now Jack! Up on him, Jack! Rear up on him and we'll settle him for once and for all! *(Roar of encouragement)* Rip him, Jack. Tear Him! Stick him! Go on Jack!

(Dinzie settles back on his chair to watch the fight. Jack draws himself up to his full height and uplifts clenched fists as a fighter will. Peadar advances immediately to Trassie and surveys her worriedly)

Trassie: *(Standing nearer to Peadar)* They were trying to catch me. He wants to hunt Neelus and myself out of the house.

Peadar: *(Determinedly)* Well, they'll never do that while I'm here, Trassie.

Dinzie: Are you going to listen to Minogue the thatcher, Jack? Minogue the robber from Glashnanaon. We heard all about you, Minogue, and the thieving breeding that's in you.

Peadar: *(Menaces)* There is no bad breeding in the Minogues. Three hundred years they farmed in Glashnanaon and never a mean or cowardly act against them; never a poor man turned away from the door; never a neighbour in want of help; never a bad word thrown out against any man.

Dinzie: Your breeding is bad! Didn't you know that a foxy-haired horse-blocker from Tipperary was the first Minogue to come to Glashnanaon? Didn't you know that he gattled a loose woman under the blind eye of Glashnanaon Bridge and that's how you came by your breeding?

Peadar: It's a roaring lie! *(Anger)* It's a holy lie, you hump-backed ferret from hell. If you were a full man, I'd break every lying bone in your body.

Dinzie: *(Thumps chair with fury)* Will you listen to him, Jack? Do you hear him? Attack him! Attack him, I say! Attack and trample the life out of him. At him, Jack.

Jack: *(Assuming fighting stance)* Come on, boy!

Peadar: *(Clenches his fists and looks calmly at Jack)* I never sought after fighting but I'll fight you and beat you if that's the way of it.

Dinzie: Go on, Jack! Give him the boot!

             (Jack circles menacingly around Peadar, who looks at him calmly)

Peadar: We won't fight in here. We'll fight outside in the open.

Dinzie: *(Fingering knife)* Fight him here, you coward. Fight him here!

Peadar: I'm no coward.

Dinzie: Fight him so!

Peadar: And have a knife between my shoulders when my back is turned to you? Give the knife to Trassie and I'll fight him here.

Dinzie: And have her stick Jack and maybe myself, a poor oul' cripple.

Peadar: Trassie wouldn't stick anybody.

Trassie: I'll stick him if he harms you, Peadar!

Peadar: *(To Jack)* Out here, if you're a man. *(Indicates the door)*

Jack: *(Fists up)* I'm not in dread of you boy. I'm not in dread of you.

Dinzie: *(Impatiently)* Give him one, Jack, I tell you! Draw one kick at him, into the stomach, and you'll do for him.

(Suddenly Jack draws a kick at Peadar but Peadar avoids it and walks towards the door. He turns to Jack with upraised finger)

Peadar: Out here, and I'll show you how to fight.

(Peadar exits)

Dinzie: After him, Jack. Give it to him hot and heavy, Jack boy. Put stones into your fists.

Jack: I'll bate him fair, Dinzie. He won't stand for long against Jack Conlee. I was never bested yet.

(Jack struts out)

Dinzie: Jack will tear him to ribbons with his bare hands. We'll settle for you then.

Trassie: He'll never beat Peadar Minogue. Peadar would beat two men.

Dinzie: The Conlees were never beat. If he beats Jack I'll give him this where 'twill sink. *(Raises knife)* I'll fool him.

Trassie: *(Advancing near Dinzie)* Would you ever think of being fair for once in your life? Have you no bit of goodness at all in you or is there nothing inside of you but evil and sin?

Dinzie: *(Violently)* Shut up! ... Shut up, I say, or I'll bury this in you.

Trassie: I'm not afraid of you! I'll warn Peadar and he'll take the knife from you. 'Tis you they'll be taking away to the home then and not Neelus. You should be in the madhouse years ago. I never in all my life saw anything as mad as you.

Dinzie: *(Erupts, and thumps chair, screams)* Shut up, I say! Shut up, or I'll dig my knife into you.

Trassie: You know 'tis the truth for me. You're a demon, a dirty sly demon and the mind is gone out of your head and there's nothing inside but sparks and flashes and frightful explosions and 'tis pity people should have for you and not fear.

Dinzie: *(Upraises his hands)* Stop! Stop! Stop! ... I'll kill you if you don't stop! I'll kill you for sure if you won't stop!

(Dinzie swings the knife wildly at Trassie. He falls from the chair to the floor but comes to balance quickly and sits on the floor. Trassie flees into corner)

(Maliciously) Come here to me! Come here, I say!

(Trassie cowers in the corner. Slowly Dinzie edges nearer)

Trassie: Keep away from me! *(Calls)* Peadar! Peadar! Peadar!

Dinzie: He's getting his due from Jack! No one to help you now, my doxie. No one to save you now. Come here to me. Come here, I say. *(Edges closer)*

Trassie: *(In terror)* Don't come near me! Don't come near me!

Dinzie: *(In triumph)* I'll give you something that'll put you screeching properly ... something that'll do your heart good.

Trassie: *(Cornered, looks about her hopelessly)* Oh, holy God, help me. *(Calls loudly)* Neelus! ... Neelus! ... Neelus! ... Help me, someone!

Dinzie: I'll help you when I get my hands on you!

Trassie: (*Kicks as Dinzie tries to catch her by leg*) Go away from me!

(*Enter Neelus*)

Trassie: Oh, thank God, Neelus. Thank God, you're here!

Neelus: (*Simply, without surprise of any kind*) What's Dinzie Conlee doing down on the floor, Trassie?

(*Dinzie slowly turns to look at Neelus for an instant, and turns to Trassie again*)

Trassie: He's trying to cut me with his knife, Neelus. Don't let him, Neelus.

Neelus: (*Advances, puzzled*) What's Peadar Minogue fighting with my cousin Jack for? You never saw such a fight, Trassie!

Trassie: (*Wearily*) Will you take the knife from Dinzie here. He has nothing in his head but killing people.

(*Neelus advances and looks down at Dinzie*)

Neelus: You can't kill Trassie!

Dinzie: (*Puzzled*) Kill Trassie? Who said anything about killing Trassie? A bit of sport I was having. What would make me kill my own dear cousin?

Trassie: Don't you believe him, Neelus. He's only fooling you. He wants to put you into the home, Neelus, and he wants to hunt you away from me for ever. You'll never be free again, Neelus.

Neelus: (*Puzzled*) Do you want to put me into a home, Dinzie?

Dinzie: (*Outraged*) Oh, good God almighty, them are the lies she's telling you. Sure don't you know well I wouldn't put you into a home, Neelus. I never heard such a story. Put me up on your back, Neelus. God bless you, boy bán, sure if I had my way 'tis around with a circus I'd send you every day of the week where you would be watching clowns and ponies no bigger than dogs. Put me up now on your back, Neelus.

Trassie: Don't do it, Neelus, he'll kill us all.

Dinzie: (Coaxing) Ah, Neelus, sure I wouldn't put a finger on one of
             my little cousins, if I got the use of my legs back again even.
             Amn't I mad about ye altogether. Yesterday week it was, I
             think, I said to Jack: Jack, says I, we must buy a pipe and
             tobacco for Neelus and train him how to smoke.

Trassie: Neelus, if you listen to him, he'll hunt you into the mad
             house.

Neelus: (Looks for a long time at Trassie, then at Dinzie, then at the
             ceiling) Would you promise me you wouldn't stick Trassie,
             Dinzie, if I put you up on my back?

Dinzie: Ah! ... I swear by all that's dead and buried belonging to me,
             I wouldn't do that!

Trassie: (Hopelessly) Oh! Don't listen to his lying tongue, my poor
             Neelus.

Neelus: I'll put you up so, Dinzie, if you promise.

             (Neelus goes on all fours on the floor. Trassie runs out from
             the corner and stands with the table between herself and
             Dinzie. Dinzie manages to get on Neelus' back. Neelus
             stands holding Dinzie tightly about his neck)

Dinzie: Get a grip on me, Neelus boy. Get a grip I say and we'll
             have sport in plenty. 'Pon my soul and conscience but
             you're every bit as good as my brother Jack.

Neelus: I'll give you a good gallop.

Dinzie: A good gallop? ... Put me down, you thunderin' pothead! ...
             Put me down, I say!

             (Suddenly Neelus twists Dinzie's hand with the knife in it
             and the knife falls. Dinzie struggles but his legs are dead
             and Neelus' grip is too strong to break with his hands)

Dinzie: Put me down, I say! *(Screeches)* Put me down! Put me down! *(Agony)* Oh, great God, take me off the back of the persecuted amadán!

Trassie: Where will you take him, Neelus?

Neelus: I'll take him for the finest gallop he ever had.

Dinzie: *(Prolonged wail)* Oooh! ... Ooooooh! ... God, take me off his back! *(Wheedling)* Put me down, Neelus, and I'll give you a lovely gold watch I have under the mattress at home. I'll give you fifty golden sovereigns I have in hiding and I'll get a handsome girl out from Lenamore to marry you if you put me down.

Neelus: *(Casual vacant)* Sure I can't, Dinzie! Sharon is waiting for me, Trassie, and Shíofra is waiting for Dinzie.

Dinzie: *(Appalled)* Shíofra ... Sharon ... He's in the power of the Devil. *(Appeals pitifully to Trassie. Screaming, struggles)* Put me down to the ground, you madman. Put me down, or I'll get Jack to kill you. Oh Lord God, put me down!

Trassie: Listen to me, Neelus! Listen to me! *(Helplessly)* Oh, dear God, my poor Neelus!

(Neelus goes towards door, carrying Dinzie)

Dinzie: *(High-pitched, terrified)* He's going to kill me in the lonely seas ... in the black hole ... I'll be dead ... *(Screams)* Put me down! ... I'll kill you! ... Kill you ... Kill you ...!

(Trassie stands motionless with horror)

Oh, sweet God, he'll drown me!

Neelus: The finest gallop you ever had.

(Neelus pulls Dinzie higher on his back and exits furiously, Trassie runs to the door calling)

Trassie: *(Tearfully)* Oh, my poor foolish Neelus, come back! Come back, Neelus! *(She extends her hands)* Neelus, come back to your own Trassie ... Neelus ... Neelus ... Come back ...

(Trassie turns, her hands covering her face. Enter Peadar, hair tossed, clothes disordered, pushing a badly-beaten cowed Jack Conlee before him. Jack's face is blood-smeared and badly bruised. Peadar dashes him to one side, into a chair, where Jack sits, head hanging stupidly, gingerly feeling his wounds)

Peadar: *(As he pushes Jack aside)* There's one man bet! Where's the other fellow? Where's Dinzie?

Trassie: Oh, Peadar! ... Peadar! ... Quick! It's Neelus ... It's Neelus and Dinzie ...!

Peadar: *(Takes her hands in his)* Easy, Trassie, girl! ... Easy! ... Easy! ... Tell me what's wrong? Take control of yourself.

Trassie: Oh, Peadar ... *(Sobs)* ... Neelus ran away with Dinzie up on his back ... *(Sobs)* ... Hurry, Peadar! Hurry, Peadar! Go after them!

(Peadar exits. Jack rises stupidly and lurches towards the door)

Jack: The thatcher bet me but he'll never beat Dinzie. *(As he lurches out the door he passes Peadar)* You'll never beat Dinzie.

Peadar: Neelus has beaten him this time. *(Pauses, then helplessly to Trassie)* He took one mighty bound like a deer and the two of them disappeared into Sharon's grave. Poor Neelus was doing his last service to us, helping the only way he knew how.

(Trassie shakes with tears, Peadar places a hand about her shoulders)

Peadar: I will look after you, Trassie. I will stay here with you always and I'll mind you. Neelus did not know what he was doing. It was to happen the way it happened. Neelus is with his own now, with his mother and father. Don't cry now, Trassie. That is the way it was cut out for us. I'm here with you for ever, Trass ...

(Trassie looks up at Peadar tenderly. Peadar takes her hand in his. She sobs and he takes her in his arms. Enter Pats Bo Bwee agitated and excited, dressed and equipped as before)

Pats: *(Delight)* We're free! We're free at last from Dinzie Conlee. Did you see the way he took him? Did you see the way Neelus ruz like a bird with him?

(Peadar edges away a little from Trassie)

'Twas always in Neelus' head to do what he did. He has his eternal reward by now. 'Tis a great thing to be free of Dinzie Conlee.

Peadar: *(Anger)* You were as much at fault as any that Neelus is dead.

Pats: *(Palm upraised, measuring Peadar carefully)* There was no other way out of it ... *(Conciliatory)* You'll settle here and you'll be wanted here. There's fresh blood wanted in here sore.

Peadar: You're a born rogue!

Pats: Musn't we all live? What have I but the one yella cow. I couldn't be raising my hand ag'in my betters.

Peadar: Get out of here!

Pats: *(Minor warning)* Ye might want me yet.

Peadar: We'll manage well without you.

Pats: *(Head cocked aside)* Will ye though? Will ye for sure? Ye'll marry now, won't ye? Ye'll marry now and think to bring a litter o' children into the world. Ye're well-blossomed the two of ye. Maybe a little too well-blossomed for children. Ye're far advanced beyond your prime.

Peadar: We'll manage.

Trassie: *(Touches Peadar's arm)* Peadar ...

Peadar: *(Indignant)* Who's he to talk? A short while ago he was
                  dead set against us. Anyway what counsel could he give that
                  never had a child of his own?

Pats: *(Knowingly)* Oooh! ... Who's to tell? ... No papers to show,
                  maybe, but they're there! *(Conspiratorially)* Ye'll want me,
                  maybe, when ye find the days gone past with no child to
                  keep ye awake at night.

Peadar: We'll manage.

Trassie: We're not getting younger, Peadar.

                  *(She links his hand. Peadar looks at her tenderly. Pats Bo
                  Bwee seizes his chance)*

Pats: After ye're wedded, wait for news of a sickle moon in the
                  sky. Ye must have the same soft will to ye for love. *(To
                  Peadar)* She must have a two o' wet lips and all of a soft-
                  ness to her. Go with her out of her warm bed at the first light
                  of day. Let ye be fond companions in the new light. Put you
                  something woollen around her for airly cold. Lie her down
                  on dewy ground with the soft wool to warm her. Face her
                  then to the first foot's fall of a flowing tide and let ye throw
                  all thoughts of worries and woes away from ye. There must
                  be a tide and ye must face the tide, a young silver tide with
                  giddy antics. *(Turns to go)* And I'll be calling within the
                  space of a year maybe to cure a blockin' of wind in a young
                  thing or to give advice about nursin'. *(Exiting, hand raised)*
                  The blessing of God attend ye. *(Exits)*

(Final Curtain)

THE CRAZY WALL

The Crazy Wall had its premiere by the Theatre of the South, Ltd., Cork at the Theatre Royal, Waterford on 27 June 1973 and subsequently opened at the Cork Opera House on 23 July, and Dublin's Gaiety Theatre, 7 May, 1974.

The cast in order of appearance were:

Paddy Barnett	Gerard Walsh
Lelum Barnett	Liam O'Mahony
Tom Barnett	Jim O'Connell
Tony Barnett	Flor Dullea
Michael Barnett, N.T., *father of the house*	Dan Donovan
Sean Trean *a carpenter*	Chris Sheehan
Jack Strong *a shoemaker*	Paddy Comerford
Lily O'Dea *the maid of the house*	Áine O'Leary
Mary Barnett *mother of the house*	Mairín Morrish
Moses McCoy *a wanderer*	James N. Healy
The voice of Lord Haw-Haw	Donal O'Donovan

DIRECTOR	Dan Donovan
DESIGNER	Patrick Murray
STAGE MANAGER	Peter Casey

ACT ONE

Scene I

Enter three young men. They are Paddy, Tom and Lelum Barnett. They wear black armbands. Winter 1963.

Paddy: It's a long time now since we were all together here.

Lelum: It's not that long. It just seems a long time. *(Lelum moves away and stands with his back turned, looking into nothingness)*

Paddy: We had good times.

Tom: They were sad times.

Paddy: Of course they were but by and large they were great old days.

Tom: It's a pity we had to break up when we did.

Lelum: *(Without turning)* All families break up. Everything breaks given enough time.

(Paddy and Tom exchange looks)

Paddy: *(Unloosing armband)* I suppose we had better take these things off.

Tom: Yes ... they serve no purpose now.

Paddy: Will I take your band Lelum?

Lelum: *(Without turning)* No. I'll leave it on a while yet.

Paddy: Let's all leave them on then.

(Enter Tony Barnett in the uniform of an army officer. He bears a tray on which is a bottle of whiskey and some glasses)

Tom: How's mother?

Tony: The girls are with her. She'll be all right.

                (Tony pours whiskey into four glasses and hands them round)

Tom: I was trying to recall as we stood by the graveside when was the last time the four of us were together in this place.

Tony: The war was at its height.

Paddy: Let's toast the memory of the man we buried today.

Lelum: *(Turning)* Yes. A toast.

Paddy: Don't you think you had better explain?

Lelum: Explain. To whom?

Paddy: To the world and to those who might be out there in the dark.

Lelum: Yes. I'd better *(To audience)* We buried our father today and so we toast his memory. To dada!

Tony: Amen.

Others: Amen.

Paddy: To outsiders he must have seemed an average man. He was anything but.

Lelum: I remember when it was that we four last stood here. It was the time of Adolf, an evil star of great magnitude whose ascendancy was brief yet long enough to bewitch his nation of Germans and stifle forever the cries of millions of mankind.

Paddy: It was the time of Musso The Wop as the British called him or Benito as his wife called him.

Tom: It was the time of Franklin Delano and Winston.

Paddy: It was the hour of Alexander and Eisenhower and Rommel and Hess, poor fellow.

Lelum: This is how history will remember it. Principally I think, when all the chaff is sifted, it will be the time of Adolf.

Paddy: But not for us four.

Tony: Oh by God no!

Lelum: For us it was the time of the crazy wall.

Paddy: That heap you see behind us.

Lelum: Erected by the man we buried today.

Paddy: Europe had it's war but we had a drama here as good as any and for us the most important drama of all.

Lelum: It made us what we are today.

Tom: The precise time we stood here together.

Paddy: Was not the night of the long knives.

Lelum: It was the night of the crazy wall.

Paddy: Judge for yourself.

Lelum: In the light of recent developments.

Tom: Which was more important.

Paddy: The rise and fall of the third Reich.

All: Or the rise and fall of the crazy wall. To dada!

(All quaff. As one they turn and fling their empty glasses against the ruins of the wall. The glasses smash to pieces)

Music: The light changes and we are in the month of May 1943. It is the late afternoon. The action takes place in the back garden of a house in the small town of Lolinn in the

*south of Ireland. It is a colourful and unruly garden with
part of the scullery of the house showing at the left facing
the audience. At the other side of the stage is an old table on
which are scattered some old paint tins, odds and ends and a
fairly large wireless set. Most of the area is ivy-coloured.
Enter a young man of twenty or so. He turns wireless dial
and flops on to an old garden seat nearby. He is of the
house. He is the second oldest son, Lelum Barnett. There is a
loud cracking from the wireless but this is superseded by the
lively martial music of a brass band. Lelum rises suddenly
and comes to attention. He salutes stiffly and marches about
like a soldier on parade. He suddenly halts and shakes his
head. From one of the shrubs he selects a flower at random,
smells it, fondles it and places it in his lapel. He returns to
his seat where he sits with his head in his hands. The music
ceases.*

Lelum: *(Perfectly mimicking voice which follows)* Station Bremen, station Bremen, Germany calling, Germany calling.

Haw-Haw: Station Bremen, station Bremen, Germany calling, Germany calling.

(Lelum Barnett sits erect and listens)

Haw-Haw: One must accord tremendous respect to the imagination of those who prepare the news bulletins in the BBC. For instance the report that the entire German army capitulated in Stalingrad is completely without foundation ....

*(Enter Michael Barnett, father of Lelum. He is a man of
fifty-five, well dressed. He is followed by two cronies. One is
bowler-hatted and sharp-faced. He is moustached and
nattily dressed. He swings a walking cane carelessly. He is
of the same age. He is Jack Strong. The third man is Sean
Trean. He is also of the same age. He is a serious-faced man
who wears the collar of his shirt outside his coat. Generally
stands with his hands behind his back, head erect, legs
apart. Michael and Sean Trean wear green armbands; these
to denote that they are members of the local defence forces.
All three would seem to be somewhat intoxicated. Their
conversation ends abruptly upon their awareness of Haw-
Haw. Michael Barnett lifts a hand for silence. All three*

range themselves around the table where the wireless sits,
having refused the offer of a seat from Lelum)

Haw-Haw: *(Continuing)* The Führer does not deny that a small part of
the German army capitulated but the truth is that the main
body of the army has left the Eastern Front for the following
reasons. It is an area not worth contesting in the light of new
developments. The Russian Front was never a priority with
the Führer. Like the British army the Russians can be beat-
en at any time.

Sean Trean: Hear, Hear.

(Michael Barnett motions for silence)

Haw-Haw: While the British army plays ducks and drakes in Tunisia the
German army occupies itself with more important develop-
ments. The truth about the British army is that it would not
beat the tinkers out of Rathkeale on a fair day.

Sean Trean: *(Beside himself)* Beautiful, beautiful. *(To Jack Strong)* Did
you hear that! The British army wouldn't beat the tinkers out
of Rathkeale.

Michael: Will you please desist or I'll turn off the damned thing.

Haw-Haw: Earlier today the Luftwaffe successfully bombed all the
major English cities. Nothing shall withstand the might of
the third Reich. It will stand for a thousand years. The invin-
cibility of German military power ...

Michael: Turn it off Lelum.

(Lelum rises and does as he is told)

What are you doing inside on a fine day like this?

Lelum: I got fed-up walking around. There's nothing to do, nowhere
to go.

Michael: You could get a job.

Lelum: There are no jobs.

Michael: *(To cronies)* I don't know what I'll do with him. There's Tony my eldest in the army, our own army. A credit to his family and to his country. There's Tom and Paddy at school, solid and predictable, and here's Lelum not knowing in God's name what he wants.

Jack: You must give him time. You can't put an old head on young shoulders.

Sean: That's a fact. We were all like him once.

Michael: If you wait another year I might manage to send you to the university.

Lelum: I've already waited a year.

Sean Trean: You could join the army. It wouldn't be for long.

Lelum: Which army?

Sean Trean: The Irish army of course.

Jack: The British would be better. At least they're fighting for something.

Lelum: They're all the bloody same. They're all fighting for their suppers. A soldier does what he's told, not what he believes.

Sean: *(Indicates his green armband)* You could join the local defence forces like us.

(Lelum and Jack Strong laugh)

Michael: Laugh if you will but we have a role to play too.

Jack: What role?

Lelum: *(To Jack)* Did you ever sit down and ask yourself what guarantees our neutrality.

Jack: Well … no. Not really.

Michael: The presence of American troops in the North guarantees it.

The proximity of England guarantees it.

Sean: The Germans respect our neutrality.

Jack: The Nazis respect nothing.

Michael: We have an army of our own remember, never stronger than it is right now.

Lelum: *(To Jack)* Did you ever ask yourself why the Russians never bother us, why England didn't take us over long ago, why the Yanks don't put an army of occupation in here? Think ... use your imagination ...

Jack: *(Pretending to let the truth dawn. Touches band on Sean's arm)* It couldn't be. You mean...

Lelum: What else? It's the green band of our local defence force my friend. That little band, small as it may be, strikes terror into the heart of every army in Europe. While men like these wear bands like those the freedom of small nations is assured. There's hope for the world, hope for us all. *(Raises his hand to salute while Jack Strong allows his hands to simulate a trumpet. He plays gently into it ... The Last Post. Sean Trean is not at all certain but that they are serious)*

Michael: Stop this nonsense at once. I'm ashamed of you Lelum. I have half a mind to strike you. And you Jack ... you should know better.

Jack: Sorry Michael. It was a poor joke. I am sorry.

Michael: You Lelum? Are you sorry?

Lelum: If that's what you want me to be.

Michael: But aren't you sorry off your own bat?

Lelum: All right. I'm sorry.

Sean: The two of you should be ashamed of yourselves. You mock your own country when you mock these bands.

Michael: Only the Irish have this peculiar ability. It's a quirk in our characters I can never fathom, this deep-rooted shame of each other's virtues, this urge to pull each other down, this mad desire to disrupt anything that's decent and good so long as it's a native creation. It's held us back for too long. I'm afraid it will always divide us.

Lelum: I said I was sorry didn't I.

Jack: A bit of criticism does no harm.

Sean Trean: Not that kind of criticism. It's no fun when our country is besmirched. Our uniforms must be revered and respected.

Michael: Easy Sean. You'll go too far the other way. That's another national failing, taking ourselves too seriously. It's hard to know which is worse … too little patriotism or too much.

Jack: The less the better.

Sean: The more the merrier.

Michael: Enough now. Let's get down to the business that brought us here.

Jack: Before we do … I think I could fix you up Lelum with a job on the county council. It's the time of the turf-cutting and they're taking on seasonal workers. Would you be interested?

Lelum: I suppose I would.

Jack: The money's good.

Lelum: In that case I'm your man. I never had enough money in my life.

Michael: Neither had I if that's what you mean. I was always short.

Lelum: Well it wasn't from giving it to me you were short.

Michael: About your business now like a good boy. We have important matters to discuss.

Lelum:	How is it you never seem to be short the price of a drink?
	(Exit Lelum)
Michael:	How does one deal with a boy like that?
Jack:	He's gone from being a boy. We shouldn't lose sight of that.
Michael:	Still that's no way to talk to his father.
Sean:	That's the new generation. They're all the same. My eldest daughter is smoking cigarettes.
Jack:	But she's a qualified nurse. She's a wage earner.
Sean:	I don't care what she is. She shouldn't smoke opposite her father.
Michael:	He's right Jack. There must be respect for authority. A line must be drawn somewhere otherwise our children could turn into dictators. But enough … let's get down to the business in hand.
Jack:	Maybe if you told us exactly what you had in mind we would be better able to advise.
Michael:	For years now, in fact since the day I was born, I've endured all kinds of trespass from neighbours, strangers, friend and foe alike. This could have been a really beautiful garden, a showpiece, but let me plant a shrub or a bed of flowers and every bloody stray ass, mule and horse in the countryside will turn up to wreck my best efforts. Take Hanratty's hens alone. The amount of damage they've done in the past twenty-five years must run into hundreds. I wouldn't mind that but if there's a bit of rivalry over a new pullet this is the arena for every cock-fight in the bloody street. Before I go any further I would like to ask you both a question and I expect an honest answer. Am I a man that looks for trouble?
Sean:	I should say not.
Jack:	A quieter man never drew breath.

Michael: Have I ever gone out of my way to provoke any person?

Both: No.

Michael: Have I ever deliberately gone in search of trouble?

Sean: Never.

Michael: I've tried peaceful means. I've spoken to Mrs Hanratty a thousand times. I've tried to reason with the owners of Strayways. I put up a sign ... trespassers will be prosecuted. I tried lettuce wire and thorny wire. All torn down. Well to come to the heel of the matter this is what I've decided. I intend to build a wall from here to here. It's the only solution.

Jack: What does the wife say?

Michael: She approves but even if she objected the wall would still go up. I intend to start right away but before I do I would like to hear your opinions. You're both tradesmen. You are also my lifelong friends.

Sean: There is no doubt but you've suffered your share. I think you're doing the right thing. You're entitled to your privacy as much as any other man.

Michael: Well Jack?

Jack: Yes, yes, you have the right. There's no gain-saying that. The bother is will it stop at one wall.

Michael: How do you mean?

Jack: One wall could lead to another if you know what I mean.

Michael: I don't know what you mean.

Jack: You build a wall. You give everybody else a licence to do the same. Soon the whole street will be full of walls. You build a wall and you keep out Hanratty's hens. You shut out stray asses, mules and horses but you also shut yourself in. Building a wall is a very serious matter. I'll concede you'll keep out undesirables. You'll have more peace and privacy but you'll also be shutting out certain other things.

Michael: What other things?

Jack: Wandering tramps, children, dogs. Even neighbours, lots of things.

Michael: Have you an alternative?

Jack: No.

Michael: Nobody will deny that I have tried every other means. I've been the very soul of reason. I have been patient. I've been tolerant. There is only one thing left and that's a wall.

Jack: If your mind is made up then you'd better build it. I don't know much about walls. I'm only a part-time shoemaker but one thing I will tell you. If you must build a wall build a right wall. Build something that will last.

Michael: I intend to. I intend to build a wall that will be standing here when our names are forgotten, a wall that will still be proof against all weathers. A wall that will stand firm and strong and indestructible when the mounds of our graves have sunk beneath the green grass. A hundred years from now a man will stop here and look and say to himself 'Christ almighty but they could build walls in those days'. That's the kind of wall I propose to build.

Jack: But you know nothing about building walls.

Michael: I know enough.

Jack: Your best bet would be to employ a stone mason.

Michael: I have no intention of employing anybody. If I can't build a simple wall after all these years then my mission in life is a failure. You are a carpenter Sean. Tell him how easy it is to build a wall.

Sean: Well it's easier than hanging a door. I believe the whole secret about building a successful wall lies in the foundation.

It's like anything. Without a foundation nothing lasts. You dig a proper foundation and you're on your way towards the building of a wall that will stand up for generations to come. A wide and deep foundation and you'll have a wall that no man need be ashamed of.

Michael: I see what you mean. You know more than you pretend Sean.

Jack: Will you lay blocks or do you propose to shore it up with boards?

Michael: No blocks for me. Who would guarantee their quality? No. I'll shore it up with boards. I'll mix the gravel and cement myself.

Sean: Make sure your gravel is well washed and of good quality. Make sure your cement is fine and dry. Make certain your level is accurate.

Michael: Your're a deep one.

Jack: He seems to know walls.

Michael: There is no part of the Atlantic ocean as deep as that man.

Sean: Just a few simple precautions, that's all.

Michael: This will be a wall to remember. I can't recall being so anxious to get started with any project.

Jack: When will you start?

Michael: I'll begin tomorrow. After school I'll open the foundations. Has anybody any other suggestions?

Jack: I think another drink would be in order.

Michael: I couldn't agree with you more. What do you say Sean?

Sean: It would be more than fitting. The wall will have to be properly baptised.

(Enter a young girl, hardly twenty. She is Lily O'Dea. She wears an apron over her frock)

Michael: Yes Lily. What is it?

Lily: The missus wants to see you Master.

Michael: Any idea what it's about Lily?

Lily: I think it's about Tom and Paddy Master.

Michael: Are they home from school?

Lily: They just come in now Master.

Michael: Tell the missus to come out here Lily. Tell her my friends are here. She'll understand.

Lily: Yes Master.

(Exit Lily)

Michael: Whenever I get started on a new scheme something always crops up to get in the way. Nothing is going to get in the way this time. No matter what, this wall is going to be built.

Jack: We can go on and you can join us later if you like.

Michael: Not at all. This won't take a minute.

(Enter Michael's wife, Mary Barnett. She's an attractive middle-aged woman. She is followed by two young men, her sons, Tom the older [17] and Paddy [16]. Both carry large, strapped bundles of school books)

What's all this in aid of?

Mary: You can prepare yourself for a shock. Your two fine sons are a nice reflection on the household.

(Lelum and Lily sidle in and range themselves in the background. Jack Strong and Sean busy themselves elsewhere on stage. Sean produces a cord, one end of which he

*hands to Jack. They measure distances, make calculations,
etc.)*

Lelum: What have they done?

Mary: You'll find out. Just read that. It's from Father Cartney.

Michael: What does that fool want? Damn well you know I don't
                  speak to him.

Mary: The letter is addressed to me but it concerns you more than
                  any of us.

(Reluctantly he accepts letter, he examines it)

Michael: I can't read this. It's worse than a bloody doctor's prescrip-
                  tion. *(To Lelum)* here. You read it. *(Lelum accepts letter)*

Lelum: *(Reading)* Dear Mrs Barnett, it is with reluctance and regret
                  but primarily because of a sense of duty that I take my pen
                  in hand to acquaint you of the doings of your sons, Thomas
                  and Patrick. As you know Tom sits for his Leaving Certifi-
                  cate this coming June and Patrick next year. Tom's teachers
                  inform me that he cannot and will not keep his eyes open
                  during classes. At first we foolishly believed that these bouts
                  of sleep might be due to the fact that he was burning the
                  midnight oil in his home but the real reason came to light at
                  two o'clock this morning. The senior curate of the parish,
                  Father Barnum, for some weeks now has been repeatedly
                  informed that some young local girls and soldiers from the
                  new barracks are misconducting themselves in Hanratty's
                  shed.

Michael: Misconducting themselves? What does he mean? Why isn't
                  he more explicit? Misconducting themselves indeed. That
                  could mean anything from piddling in public to free-handed
                  fornication.

Mary: Will you please let Lelum read on.

Michael: It's a wonder the oul' gasbag wouldn't call a spade a spade.

Mary: Go on Lelum.

Lelum:	*(Reads on)* Father Barnum lay in hiding for a while and when he heard singing and laughter in the shed he decided to inform Mr and Mrs Hanratty. The Hanratty's with the aid of a storm lamp and accompanied by Father Barnum entered the shed unannounced and witnessed a number of local serving girls lying in the hay with soldiers. Also in the shed was your son Thomas who stands for his Leaving Certificate this year. He had his arms around a girl. He ran off when the light was shone on him, knocking Mrs Hanratty to the ground. This in itself was just one offence and, serious as it was, might be overlooked on his undertaking to turn over a completely new leaf but the simple truth is that he goes to the shed repeatedly and according to Mrs Hanratty his voice can be heard clearly above all the others at all hours of the morning.
Michael:	Is this true Tom? ... Is it true? For the last time Tom is it true?
Tom:	Yes.
Michael:	But what about your exam?
Tom:	I'm sorry dada.
Michael:	But how did you get out of the house? The front and back doors were locked and bolted.
Tom:	I tied a rope to the leg of the bed and scaled down the front of the house.
Lelum:	The call of the wild.
Michael:	You shut up. Tom, this is a terrible admission. You've betrayed us all, me, your mother, your brothers and sisters. You've cheapened us in the eyes of our neighbours and disgraced yourself. We pay dearly for your education. We feed and clothe you and this is how you repay us. I don't know what to say to you. Nothing I could do to you would be punishment enough.
Mary:	He should be whipped and kicked 'till his bones ache. He deserves nothing but contempt. 'Twill be many a long day

before I speak to him again.

Michael: What have you to say for yourself?

Tom: I'm sorry.

Mary: If he says that once more I'll split him.

Tom: *(Anguish)* What else can I say? I'm sorry. I'm really sorry that I should disgrace you all.

Michael: Go to bed Tom.

(Tom bends to collect his books)

Leave your books. Go to bed and stay in your room until I call you.

(Tom is about to exit)

Tom: Can I have my supper before I go?

Michael: *(Suddenly losing temper)* Jesus I'll give you supper in the arse if you don't move out of here fast.

(As he advances upon Tom the latter exits hastily)

Mary: Is that all?

Michael: That's all for now.

Mary: Get your walking stick and go after him. Beat him within an inch of his life. He deserves it. Go after him and beat him. That's what he understands.

Michael: It's not over yet. I'll deal with him later.

Mary: Later, later. It's always later. One day it will be too late. Well, he's not going to escape me. If you don't beat him I will.

(She seizes a stick from table and exits. She is followed by a gasping Lily)

Michael:	*(Futilely follows her a few paces)* Now, now Mary. You mustn't upset yourself. Beating him will achieve nothing. *(He turns away hopelessly)* Why did it have to be our Tom. Just when everything was going so smoothly. Just when I thought I was on top of the world. We never know what's in store for us from one minute to the next.
Jack:	Don't let it upset you Michael. The rearing of a family has it's ups and downs.
Sean:	That's the truth. If you could remember that it's only all going through life. That it will even itself out in the end. What seems awful now will be nothing in the course of time.
Jack:	For every bad day there's a good day.
Sean:	For every frown there's a smile.
Jack:	For every tear a laugh. It's the balance of life.
Michael:	You're a consolation boys. A pure consolation. That boy was reared better than any in the street and what good does it do? *(He notices Paddy and remembers that he too is mentioned in dispatches)* And pray what perversion has this misbegotten wretch perpetrated when our backs were turned?
Lelum:	*(Lifts letter aloft and laughs)* This is absolutely priceless. This is the sort of thing that belongs in Hans Andersen. This is the sort of thing that could happen only to a product of this environment – in short my dear father it could only happen to a son begotten by you.
Michael:	Read the letter and don't be so pass remarkable.
Lelum:	*(Reads)* Consequently for the good of the class I am suspending your son Thomas Barnett for a period of one week.
Michael:	I see nothing priceless about that. That's bloody hard luck with his exam only a month away.
Lelum:	It's not that. It's our friend here.

Michael: What about him?

Lelum: *(Reads)* So much for your son Thomas and I am indeed sorry Mrs Barnett that the suspension has to take place. For the sake of good order in the school I have no other course open to me. With regard to the younger boy Paddy I don't quite know where to begin. In the middle of his Greek class less than a month ago he excused himself and went outside presumably to answer a call of nature. When he did not return after a quarter of an hour his teacher became suspicious and decided to investigate. He found your son Paddy talking to himself on the elevated stone steps near the lavatory at the rear of the school. When asked what he was doing he replied that he was invoking the aid of the holy ghost as he was about to embark on the writing of an epic poem. Since then his teachers can get no good out of him. He has been warned repeatedly. His final exam comes up next year as you know and this is hardly the type of groundwork that is conducive to good results. Rather than suspend him I would ask you and his father to speak to him and point out to him the error of his ways. I am indeed astonished at the father's blindness to the doings of his sons, moreover since he is a teacher himself. I dare not communicate with him knowing his irrational dislike of me. This is why I write to you my dear Mrs Barnett. Sincerely yours, Reverend Philip Cartney. B.A. H.DIP., President, Saint Martin's College, Lolinn.

Michael: For the life of me I don't know how some of these fellows get into the church, bloody refugees from the troubles of the world, hidden behind the smokescreen of holy orders.

Sean: He writes a good letter.

Michael: He has nothing better to do. *(Turns to Paddy)* What in the name of God has gotten into you? What are you? A shagging half-wit? What's this nonsense about epics?

Paddy: I started it three weeks ago.

Michael: Don't you know you damned fool that all the good poetry has been written.

Paddy: An epic is different.

Michael: What about your exam?

Paddy: That's not until June twelve months.

Sean: What's an epic?

Jack: Some sort of long poem.

Sean: Poetry is bad enough without having it long.

Jack: Still there should be some respect for it.

Michael: What's this epic about? *(All gather round)*

Paddy: I'd rather not say.

Michael: Please don't prevaricate with me. What's the theme?

Paddy: All right. Picture a green field under a low-lying, cloudy sky. These clouds are wild and uncontrollable as they tumble across the great prairies of the heavens. They are charged with electricity with the result that you have an atmosphere of supercharged tension all around the field.

Michael: The epic is about a field?

Paddy: No. It's about a football field and about a match which took place on it.

Michael: What match?

Paddy: A challenge match.

Michael: A challenge match between who?

Paddy: Between Ballybobee and Ballybobawn.

                (All laugh except Paddy)

Michael: Oh sweet Jesus that suffered for us. Tell me I'm hearing things.

Lelum: Ballybobee and Ballybobawn. Those teams are so bad that they're not even accepted in the junior league.

Paddy: Maybe not but they take their football seriously. It's like a religion with them.

Michael: Those drunken bastards couldn't play football if they were paid. They're the biggest blackguards and the vilest thugs in the country.

Paddy: Only where football is concerned. You'll have to concede that.

Michael: Granted. But what a subject for an epic. How many lines have you written?

Paddy: Nearly a thousand.

Michael: Iambic pentameter naturally.

Paddy: Naturally.

Michael: How many more thousand do you propose to write?

Paddy: Oh … I should do it in twenty thousand lines all told.

Michael: How long will it take you?

Paddy: A year and a half, maybe two years.

Michael: And what about your exam?

Paddy: This is more important than any exam.

Michael: I have news for you my friend. You will abandon this epic at once and concentrate on your studies.

Lelum: You know when you come to think about it it's not a bad idea. The last time those two teams met in a football match the referee was all but murdered.

Jack: I remember that. The spectators fought for four hours after the game.

Lelum: Nineteen were taken to hospital including three women.

Jack: A man died a few months after as a result of a kick in the head.

Paddy: That's it. These teams are prepared to kill for football. They're prepared to die if needs be. That's why it has to be an epic. Can't you see it? The air of dreadful tension before the game, the supporters screaming for blood. The teams take the field. Suddenly the sky opens and old Mars himself, the great god of war, steps forth to start the game. He raises his hands aloft to the heavens and they respond with a fearful crack of thunder. That is the signal. The game is on and Ballybobee break away. The crowd goes berserk as the Ballybobawn backs absorb the first assault. The ball lands at midfield and Micky Donovan has it. He cuts through the Ballybobee defence like a scythe through switch grass. He takes a shot and the wind whips the ball aloft. It falls in the goal-mouth. There is a melee. Boots and fists fly. Blood flows free and men lie groaning in the square but the ball is in the net and it's a goal, a great goal for Ballybobee. The ball is placed for the kickout ...

Michael: That will do.

Paddy: The ball is placed for the kick-out.

Michael: I said that will do. Enough of this infernal nonsense. Take your books and get into the house.

                (Takes books and is about to depart)

                And listen my friend ... another single solitary line of poetry of any kind during the school term and your mother won't know you when I'm done with you. I'm not finished yet. Yourself, Tom and you Lelum will join the local defence forces forthwith. Discipline is what you all need and by God you're going to get it. Now get out of here before I forget we live in a civilised country.

                (Exit Paddy)

Lelum: You're a notorious bluffer. Talking is not going to stop him.

I know Paddy.

Michael: I'll be the best judge of what's right for Paddy. *(To Jack and Sean)* Gentlemen I think it's time we had that drink.

Jack: *(Rubbing his hands together)* High time indeed. *(Extends courtesy of first exit to Sean)* After you Sean. Sail before steam. There will be no breach of maritime law while I'm aboard.

Sean: So long Lelum.

Lelum: So long Sean.

(Exit Sean)

Jack: So long Lelum. I'll fix that job for Monday.

Lelum: Thanks Jack.

(Exit Jack)

Michael: *(Indicates local defence force band on his arm)* In a few days you'll be wearing one of these. You'll be serving your country at last. *(Exit Michael)*

Lelum: I can't wait to see myself in uniform.

(Curtain)

ACT ONE

Scene II

*Action as before. The time is the afternoon of a week later. Brilliant
sunshine. The wireless plays lazy 1940s tunes in the background. The scene
has changed slightly. Seated on the garden seat is Mary Barnett. Lelum
wears the band of the local defence forces on his arm. In the background
are the upright shoreboards which will encase the wall. Lelum is seen to be
looking down into the aperture between the boards. He moves to where
there is a mixture of cement and gravel and touches same with his shoe.*

Lelum: If he doesn't come back soon this stuff will be gone hard.
Where did he go anyway?

Mary: To the river for more gravel.

Lelum: What a wall this is going to be.

Mary: Come here Lelum and hold this yank of wool for me.

*(He sits on the seat and extends his hands. She entwines the
hank round them and starts to make a ball of thread)*

Lelum: I think he's using the wall to avoid reality.

Mary: I suppose in a way you're right but we're all the same aren't
we? We all need something to hide behind at times. You and
he don't seem to be hitting it off lately. I think you're under
the impression he's failed you.

Lelum: Well hasn't he?

Mary: You mean because he didn't send you to the university?

Lelum: Among other things.

Mary: If you were an only son Lelum or if there were only two or
even three of you the university would be no problem but
there are four of you and then there are the girls. You don't
know how lucky you are to have received a secondary education. When I was a girl only one in a hundred was so

lucky.

Lelum: If he didn't drink so much.

Mary: He doesn't drink that much and when he does it's only in spasms. He works hard. Apart from the teaching there are the private tuitions. It's mostly the tuition money he drinks. He's never refused me anything. We don't know what hunger is. We have a fine home.

Lelum: I don't know what to do. I've no job.

Mary: You have your job in the bogs.

Lelum: We both know there's no future there. Anyway there's only another month of it.

Mary: You'll get a job and what's more you'll get a good job. You have brains Lelum and you're a good worker. You're young and strong and you're good looking. It's only a matter of time.

Lelum: I know what I'd really like to do but I'm almost afraid to say it.

Mary: You can say it to me. That's as far as 'twill go. Come on Lelum. You and I are too fond of each other to have secrets.

Lelum: Well ... I'd like to become a professional actor ... aren't you going to laugh?

Mary: Why would I laugh?

Lelum: Nobody from this town ever became a professional actor.

Mary: I should think that would be a reflection on the town.

Lelum: You mean you'd approve?

Mary: If it's what you really want Lelum I approve. I'll do all in my power to help you. Have you done anything about it?

Lelum: I spoke to Mr McMaster the last time he was here and he promised me an audition this time round. They'll be in town next week.

Mary: What will the audition consist of?

Lelum: A piece of my own choice from Shakespeare. I've ordered a copy of *Romeo and Juliet* from a book shop in Dublin. I'll do the balcony scene.

Mary: That would be marvellous.

Lelum: What about himself?

Mary: You picked an unfortunate profession. He hates actors.

Lelum: I know. I've heard him.

Mary: According to him they're all idlers and seducers.

Lelum: There's more to it than that.

Mary: Of course there is. He once loaned five pounds to an actor. He was a member of a touring company. He never got it back. Then his first girlfriend was stolen from him by an actor who was also a member of a touring troupe.

Lelum: Better say nothing then.

Mary: Not for the present. You go ahead with your plans. We'll work it out. You know ... I think you'd make a marvellous actor. There's something about you. I acted in a play once, *The Colleen Bawn.*

Lelum: I think the gravel-seekers are back.

Mary: Not a word about acting.

               (Enter Michael Barnett with a shovel on his shoulder. He is followed by Tom and Paddy wearing green armbands. Tom pushes a wheelbarrow full of gravel. He stops exhausted)

Tom: *(To Paddy)* It's your turn. *(Tom flops on a seat) Paddy pushes wheelbarrow across stage and empties it near the wall)*

Paddy: Where do you want it?

Michael: Let me see now ... I think you might leave it in the outhouse for the present.

(Exit Paddy pushing barrow. At once Michael goes to the heap of gravel and cement and commences to mix it. He finds a bucket and goes to a water barrel. He returns to the heap and pours some water on it. He mixes furiously with the shovel, whistling happily)

Mary: I think I'll go for a walk. I promised the girls I'd take them to the river. Are you coming Lelum?

Lelum: Yes I'll go with you.

Mary: Would you like a cup of tea Michael before I go?

Michael: *(Without looking round)* No thanks. You go off and take the air. I can't afford to fall behind. That's why I must take advantage of every fine day.

Mary: Very well. We'll be off then. Don't overdo it Michael. Rome wasn't built in a day.

(Exit Mary and Lelum. Michael continues to mix industriously. Seeing his opportunity Tom rises and tiptoes to exit. He is about to depart)

Michael: Where do you think you're going?

Tom: *(Surprised)* Nowhere. Nowhere at all.

Michael: Get your books and start revising.

Tom: Now?

Michael: Now.

(Tom locates books under the table and selects a few. Enter Paddy)

Paddy: I left the wheelbarrow in the outhouse. I have to be off now. I'll see you all later. *(Heads to exit)*

Michael:	Come back here. Get out your books and get down to work.

(Reluctantly Paddy locates books under the table and selects one at random. He sits near Tom. Michael shovels mixture into the bucket and goes to the wall)

In future as well as night time studies there will be afternoon studies. *(They begin to expostulate)* I want no arguments. *(He pours buckets contents into shored boards and locates a trowel with which he arranges mixture inside. He adds an adjacent stone or two)*

Paddy: I wonder what Homer's father said when he announced he was writing an epic?

Tom: He gave him every encouragement.

Paddy: Why do you say that?

Tom: Homer wrote the *Odyssey* didn't he? He wrote the *Iliad.* You don't write *Odysseys* and *Iliad*s without help from your father. I can see old Homer senior patting the young fellow on the back and boasting about him to the neighbours ... That's my son. He's the boy that writes the epics. He plays football as well.

Michael: Listen here you two, one more word and I'll send the pair of you to bed. How would you like that?

(The pair show exaggerated attention to the books. Enter Lily)

Lily: There's a man to see you Master.

Michael: What kind of man Lily?

Lily: He's not an insurance agent anyway Master.

Michael: How can you be sure?

Lily: Well he has a whisker Master and a bag on his back.

Michael: Then he can't be a process server either. Better send him on in Lily.

Lily: Yes Master.

          (Exit Lily)

Michael: Probably some poor devil with some sort of form to fill. *(More to himself)* Could be some relation of the wife's of course.

          (Enter a severely bearded man wearing an old hat and carrying a bag on his back. He would be in his late fifties or thereabouts. He is Moses McCoy)

Moses: *(To Michael)* Good day to you sir.

Michael: Good day to you too sir. What can I do for you?

Moses: Are you Barnett the schoolmaster?

Michael: The very man. Come on in and take a seat. Would you like a cup of tea?

Moses: *(Moving in)* No thank you Master. I have here a drop that does me more good than tea. *(He produces a bottle and takes a swig)*

Moses: I suppose 'twould be no good asking you to have a drop of this Master?

Michael: I'm partial to all kinds of drink. What is it?

Tom: It smells like methylated spirits.

Michael: In that case you'll forgive me if I decline. It's a beverage I don't care for. How can I help you?

Moses: I have here a form to fill Master.

Michael: What kind of form?

Moses: 'Tis for the claiming of money and property.

Michael: British army?

Moses: Yes Master. *(He produces bottle again)*

Michael: That stuff will poison you. Put if away and we'll have a decent drink. *(To Tom)* Get a jug from Lily and go down to Hogans for a half gallon of porter. Tell Hogan I'll square up at the end of the month.

(Tom rises and makes for exit)

You tell Hogan it's for me personally, that I want pure porter, not slops or drippings. It must be direct from the wood and take none yourself. I'll smell your breath when you come back just in case.

Tom: *(Digesting instructions)* A half gallon of pure porter ... direct from the wood ... drink none myself.

Michael: Will you get along.

(Exit Tom)

Have you got the form on you?

Moses: Yes Master. I have it here. *(He withdraws a crumbled form from his pocket. He hands it to Michael. Michael studies it carefully)*

Moses: *(To Paddy)* What's he building there?

Paddy: It's a wall.

Moses: For what?

Paddy: Privacy.

Moses: Are you and the other chap his sons?

Paddy: That's right.

Moses: I had sons once and I had a wife. She was a grand girl with red hair. She was tall too and slender like a willow. My sons were like giants. You never saw their likes.

Paddy: What happened?

Moses: *(Points a finger upwards)* Mr so-called God. *(Shakes fist upward)* Mister blind God that one day I'll catch up with *(Insanely)* and strangulate and tear apart and crush to mincemeat. He'll answer to me when I meet him.

Paddy: Nearly everyone says God is good.

Moses: Only people that lost nothing says that. God is not good and was never good. If he was good he wouldn't spend most of the time with his back turned, with his fingers in his ears and his eyes closed. God is cold and cruel. He gave us life all right but he gave us no means of keeping it. Don't talk to me about God.

Michael: *(Looking up from form)* The total financial belongings of both boys amounts to thirty-one pounds seven and three pence. Your full name is Moses McCoy?

Moses: That is so Master.

Michael: *(Sits in place vacated by Tom. He writes on form)* What's your present address?

Moses: I have none.

Michael: I'll put you care of myself or some post office. Say which.

Moses: Care of yourself Master.

(Michael writes on form)

Michael: Now … your wife's maiden name?

Moses: Sheila Summertree.

Michael: She will also have to sign this you know.

Moses: She's dead.

Michael: I'm sorry.

Moses: It wasn't your fault. It was Mister so-and-so bloody God.

Michael: Bad enough losing your sons but your wife as well ... is she long dead?

Moses: She died the fourth of January eight years ago when there wasn't a leaf on a tree or a sign of sunlight. Consumption was the boy that took her but he was sent by God.

Michael: Where did the boys die?

Moses: El Alamein. The two together. A shell.

Michael: Quite a few from around here were in the eighth army. They all died. Some died at El Alamein. Others at Tobruk. They were little more than children when they left. What is your present occupation?

Moses: You can put down I'm a wanderer.

Michael: I can but it might hold up the money.

Moses: I used to be a labouring man. Then the wife was taken. Then the boys. I sold the cottage and went through the money in a few months.

Michael: Drink?

Moses: What else? Marriage is a great thing Master until the partner is taken.

Michael: Marriage is the only true drama Moses. The moods, the conflicts, the love are paramount throughout. Unfortunately, like all great drama it must end in tragedy when one of the principals bows out forever. I'll put down your occupation as labourer. *(Writes)* What is your age?

Moses: Fifty-six.

Michael: Your religion?

Moses: *(Violently)* None.

Michael: Into what religion were you born?

Moses: I don't remember being baptised but I was confirmed a Catholic.

Michael: Catholic it is then. I think I have all I need here. We'll have to have a witness of course. Sign here Paddy.

(Paddy accepts pen and signs)

Now Moses. If you will be good enough to sign here.

(Moses arrives at table)

As you will see the money amounts to thirty-one pounds seven shillings and three pence. Both boys had watches, fountain pens and other odds and ends. The watches were stolen but the other stuff will be sent on. Write across here. *(Hands him pen. Moses signs)*

Moses: Will I have long to wait?

Michael: They're most efficient in the British war department. Not more than a week I would say. I'll hold the letter for you.

Moses: Do that Master and we'll have a good long drink.

(Enter a flustered Lily in a hurry followed by Tom bearing a gallon. Lily runs behind table while Tom re-arranges hair and endeavours to look composed)

Michael: What's this about?

Tom: What's what about?

Michael: Has he interfered with you in any way Lily?

Lily: No Master. No.

Michael: Are you sure?

Lily:	Yes Master. Yes, yes.
Michael:	All right Lily. Bring a few glasses.
Lily:	Yes Master.

(Exit Lily)

Michael: *(To Tom)* You sit down. *(Tom does so)* You're a man that's causing me great concern lately. So much so that I'll have to take serious steps to chastise you.

(Enter Lily bearing glasses. These she places on the table and exits silently)

(Tom and Paddy go back to their books)

(Michael hands a glass of porter to Moses, who thanks him, and takes a glass himself)

I toast this wall which you see before you. May it stand when the names of Hitler and Mussolini are erased from the memories of mankind.

(All quaff)

(Replenishing glass which he has emptied at one swallow. To Tom) There is something you had better know about women my friend.

Tom: *(Keenly interested as is Paddy)* Yes dada.

Michael: Any sort of extreme involvement with members of the opposite sex can be most dangerous, even fatal. *(To Tom)* Remember that every time you think about, talk to, kiss or caress a woman your heart beats at several times the normal speed. Now the heart has only so many beats and when these are exhausted there is that awful struggle for breath, that ultimate cry of anguish and despair and finally that last terrible gasp. *(Swallows porter and refills his glass. Lelum does likewise for himself and Moses. To Tom)*

If by merely thinking about women the heart beats faster imagine the speed if a man makes total love to a woman. It is not so bad for an old man as his heart is bigger and better developed but a young heart, say that of a man in his teens, cannot possibly stand up to the strain of repeated strong courting and loving. He is wasting beats by the thousand and bringing on a sudden and untimely death. Every time you put your hands around a woman days, weeks, months are dropping from your life's span. It is my opinion Tom that unless you completely change your attitude towards the opposite sex you will die in your sleep one night very soon and then will come that awful day when your brothers and I will bear you from this house in a coffin and lay you to rest in a grave that is deep and dank and final. Maybe you think that is bad. That's only the beginning my friend for next will come that awful confrontation with your maker. He will ask you certain questions and when you have rendered an account for every single moment you spent on this earth he will pass sentence. Knowing you Tom and knowing of your past misdeeds there is only one place he can send you and Tom believe me when I say it is a spot where you'll see no angels and where you'll never be troubled with the cold. The next time you feel inclined to catch a hold of poor Lily think of that last awful encounter with your God.

Moses: *(Jumps up suddenly and screams)* God is a cheat and a coward. God is a murderer. *(Challenging stance)* Come out God. Come out God wherever you are and face me like a man. Give me back the wife and sons you stole from me. *(Prances around shadow boxing furiously)* Give me what's mine you cruelty man, you stinking, two-faced hypocrite that hides away whenever he's asked to relieve our misery. You're worse than the devil. It was you who created us. The devil never created anything except what you made for him. Come out I tell you 'till I see you. Come out you coward.

(He flings empty glass against wall where it smashes)

Michael: My wall. My wall. What are you doing to my wall. In the name of God catch hold of him before he knocks what I've built.

(Tom and Paddy subdue him)

Michael:	It's the bloody methylated spirits. Hold him down. Hold him.
Paddy:	I think he's all right now. Are you all right now?

(Moses nods his head. He is seated on the ground flanked by Tom and Paddy. Paddy lets go of his hold of Moses' neck. Tom also releases hold on his legs)

Michael:	He seems to be subdued. Why in God's name did he fling the glass at the wall? Why not the table or the seat or the gable end of the house? Why not the outhouse? Why the wall?
Paddy:	It could be a plot.
Michael:	A plot?
Paddy:	Don't you see? Word of this wall has already spread far and wide. There's bound to be jealousy. There could be a conspiracy to sabotage it.
Michael:	Your particular brand of sarcasm will land you in serious trouble some day.

(Paddy and Tom help Moses to his feet)

Moses:	I'm sorry Master. I don't know what came over me.

(Lily enters with potatoes which she deposits on the table preparatory to peeling. She then exits to the kitchen)

(Tom hands Moses his hat which fell off during the struggle)

Moses:	When I think that I'll never see my wife or sons again I lose the head. Soon I'll put a finish to it all.
Michael:	Don't say that.
Moses:	My mind is made up. I've it planned a long time now.
Michael:	Time will straighten you out my friend.

Moses: If I had the money from the war department drank I'd go about it.

Lelum: Give the world a chance awhile yet. It's not as bad as you think.

Michael: I think what we need is a drink. I don't feel like going back to the wall just yet. *(To Paddy)* Do you happen to have any money on you?

Paddy: I have five shillings.

Michael: That's plenty. *(To Moses)* Bring your bag. You'll feel better after a pint of porter. *(To Tom and Paddy)* You two get back to work.

(Exit Moses followed by Michael)

Michael: *(Exiting – to Moses who has just exited)* I always say there is no sanctum like a public house when pressures begin to mount. *(To Paddy and Tom)* Get back to your studies. In precisely thirty minutes take the wheelbarrow and bring a load of gravel from the river. Choose it well. I want no big stones and I want no mud. I want the stones to be small and of uniform size and I want the wheelbarrow full because when I come back I propose an all-out assault. Diversions such as we've experienced only serve to strengthen my resolve. Before the hot breath of August blows down the year that fragment of wall you see before you will stretch from there to there, rock-like and enduring, a finished work, in it's own right a masterpiece.

(Curtain)

ACT TWO

Scene I

Action as before. This time in the afternoon of a week later. The wall has been extended a little although no great progress has been made. Michael Barnett is busily affixing scraps of plaster to that part of the wall which has been completed. Seated close by is his wife Mary. She is knitting a pullover.

Michael: What do you think of it?

Mary: It's a bit early for comment yet.

Michael: Still you must have some opinion.

Mary: It seems all right but then I'm no judge of walls.

Michael: You think it's all right?

Mary: *(Putting aside knitting rises and examines the wall from one end)* I hate to say this and I hate to have to be the one to tell you because no one else would dare but it seems a little bit crooked.

Michael: Where?

Mary: *(Points)* There. In the middle and it seems to have sunk a bit here.

Michael: Those faults are so minor that they are inconsequential. I more or less followed my instincts from the outset. If it is a shade crooked and if it has sunk a little that's all for the best. What it means is that the wall is merely following the natural contours of the place where it stands. It's a perfectly natural development. It's not perfect. None of us is. The idea from the beginning was the erection of a wall that would last. I never intended to build a showpiece. All I had in mind was a wall that would endure.

Mary: Of course. I wouldn't have said it at all but I thought you hadn't noticed.

Michael: Of course I noticed.

Mary: Well ... having said what I had to say I think it's going to be a fine wall.

Michael: *(Standing back to admire his handiwork)* I think so too.

Mary: *(Returns and resumes her knitting)* I'm worried about the boys Michael.

Michael: They're no different to any other boys of the same age.

Mary: Oh but they are. They're headstrong.

Michael: What boy isn't?

Mary: They are at the age where it's difficult to talk to them and more difficult to handle them. If ever a boy deserved a hiding it was Tom. You left yourself down badly there.

Michael: He hasn't been to the hayshed since.

Mary: How can you be sure?

Michael: He promised me.

Mary: If you gave him the beating of his life when he deserved it there wouldn't be any need for promises and look at Paddy. We both know in our hearts that he's writing poetry non-stop.

Michael: Deep down I feel that it's wrong to stop a boy from writing poetry. That's down deep. I realise of course that it will have to stop for the moment. I think it has and I think there's no need to say any more. I know he dabbles away at it but dammit we don't want to kill his interest altogether.

Mary: You'll always find excuses. Then there's Lelum. He's anxious to get started in life, to make some sort of career for himself. You'd badly want to sit down and have a long talk with him.

Michael: I think I might manage to send him to the university this coming October.

Mary: When did you change your mind?

Michael: I've been thinking about it for some time and I think it can be done. It will mean giving up the drink but that might be no harm.

Mary: That's great entirely but the bother is he may not want to go to a university.

Michael: Then what the hell does he want?

Mary: If you took the trouble to listen sympathetically, you'd encourage him to tell you about his hopes and his fears and his doubts but you won't do that.

Michael: Beneath all the banter Lelum and I have a great love for each other. It's the same with the other two.

Mary: I know, but if they feared you more and respected you more it might be better for themselves. Sometimes instead of treating you like a father they treat you like a brother.

Michael: What's wrong with that?

Mary: You are their father and it's your duty to drive them, to bully them, to forge them into men. You should be completely in command but you're not and they know you're not. When my brothers were their ages they dare not raise their voices, dare not contradict. They were afraid of their sacred lives of my father. Yet he hardly gave them three beatings in their lives but by God when he did it was years before they needed another. It was unpleasant and there was an atmosphere of horrible unrest in the house afterwards but signs on they are all well-adjusted, happy men today and to make men like that you must face up to the full responsibility of fatherhood no matter how unpleasant it may be. You must check up on your sons, spy on them if necessary for their own good. You must keep on their heels relentlessly if they are to grow up decently.

Michael: I work hard with them. I'm always in touch.

Mary: In touch yes but never at grips. You won't look under the surface because you're afraid of what you'll see.

Michael: You want me to be inquisitorial?

Mary: A father has the power and the right.

Michael: If I look under the surface all I'll see is myself and all my weaknesses and that's not a pleasant sight. Essentially they're good boys, I love them and I am not going to dissect or analyse them. Let the world outside do that. That's what the world is for. You can only go so far with your children.

Mary: That sounds good but it's not the right way. Most of the other boys in the street ...

Michael: Most of the other boys in the street are being swept along with most of the other boys in the country. They have their standards and these standards do not allow them to think for themselves. It might jeopardise their exam chances or their civil service jobs if they acted differently from the main herd. Jesus that would never do.

Mary: You want the boys to be different.

Michael: I do and I don't. I want them to be aware of things, not to be insensitive and unconcerned. I am not going to whip them along with the main herd.

Mary: They'll be stragglers then.

Michael: Yes but they'll be observers too and they'll see what the herd is really like and they'll be fortunate in that they'll see that there is a world outside the herd.

Mary: I'm no match for you.

Michael: Oh yes you are when it suits you but on this occasion in your heart of hearts you agree with me.

Mary: In a sense but I don't want my sons to be freaks.

Michael: They won't be. They'll feel. They'll record. They'll be conscious when others are deliberately unconscious.

Mary: Do you know that Tom never stops making passes at Lily?

Michael: I don't think you need have any more worries on that score. I gave him a right talking to last week.

Mary: Lily is not the brightest you know.

Michael: I don't know what to say.

Mary: Say nothing. Just get your walking cane and make him so sore that he'll have something else to think about. Sometimes you make me sick. You close your eyes when there's a problem. Honestly there are times when I'm disgusted with you. You leave all the dirty work to me. I have to worry about the bills, about the future, about everything. When things get difficult you go and build a wall. That's your answer when your family really needs firm direction.

(Enter Lily)

Lily: Mister Trean and Mister Strong is outside Master.

Michael: Send them right in Lily. *(Exit Lily. He looks at his watch)* It's almost time for Haw-Haw.

Mary: You'll grasp at any straw rather than face up to your real responsibilities.

Michael: Mary mo chroí the world isn't worth all the attention you'd have me to give it. Be satisfied that you and I are still in love. If the world had it's way we wouldn't be.

Mary: I suppose I'd better try and be content with my lot. There's no use arguing with you. You're beyond redemption.

(Enter Jack Strong and Sean Trean. They exchange pleasantries with Mary)

(To all) I have things to do.

Sean: Don't say we're the cause of your going.

Mary: Indeed you're not Sean. I have to get the girls ready for bed.
                 'Bye all.

                 *(Exit Mary. Michael goes to wireless and turns knob. Almost
                 at once there is a loud blast of martial brass. He modifies
                 sound)*

Michael: What's new?

Sean: Father Barnum denounced Hanratty's hay shed at devotions
                 last night.

Michael: You're not serious?

Sean: From now on it's out of bounds for soldiers.

Jack: I don't know if that's wise. Soldiers have to have women.

Sean: That's absolutely heinous.

Jack: What is?

Sean: To make a vile charge like that against the Irish army.
                 They're not like the soldiers of other countries. They don't
                 need women.

Jack: You mean they're not endowed with ...

Sean: I'm saying that this is a Catholic country.

Michael: Easy now. It's on news time. *(He raises volume. Lelum
                 enters)*

Haw-Haw   Station Bremen. Station Bremen. Germany calling. Ger-
                 many calling. Good evening ladies and gentlemen and what
                 a lovely evening it was in London until the sirens sounded
                 the arrival of countless waves of German bombers. This
                 bombing is a mere picnic compared to what the British can
                 expect when the new German secret weapon descends like
                 an avenging angel from the heavens. Against it there can be
                 no defence.

                 (Enter Paddy and Tom bearing strapped parcels of books.

They gather round)

The recent British announcement that all German resistance in North Africa has ended is causing genuine and prolonged laughter to the German people. The withdrawal of all German forces from the worthless deserts of the dark continent is merely part of the great counter offensive against Russia.

Sean: Hear, hear. *(Claps his hands)*

Haw-Haw: Our panzer divisions are re-grouping and soon these inexorable units aided by a new terrible weapon will ring the death knell for the allies. The cities of Britain will be bombed out of existence.

Sean: Proper bloody order.

Michael: Silence sir.

Haw-Haw: Consequently the British announcement that all German resistance in North Africa is crushed can be seen as another fairy tale. It is the wish of the Führer that the real war now commence on the East European front where twenty panzer divisions will annihilate the starving armies of Russia.

Michael: Turn it off. *(Tom does so at once)*

Lelum: I wonder if they've really got a secret weapon.

Sean: You can be sure of it.

Jack: Every Irish soldier has the same secret weapon, only waiting for the chance to use it.

Sean: You mock the tradition of the Fianna who revered and venerated the purity of Irish womanhood ... you belittle the noble heritage of the Irish fighting man.

Michael: Now ... now ... now. *(He proceeds to mix cement and gravel)* Let there be no more arguing. *(To Paddy and Tom)* You two go in and have your supper. Then straight to your books.

Jack: *(To Tom)* Did you hear Hanratty's hay shed was denounced from the pulpit?

Tom: *(Righteously)* I know nothing about that place. I never go near it now.

Jack: It's been put out of bounds to soldiers and it's to be locked and barricaded from now on.

Tom: That has nothing to do with me.

Lelum: Of course not. Everybody knows that. *(Mockery to Jack)* How dare you suggest that this man would demean himself by visiting such a place.

Tom: *(To Lelum)* Watch it.

Lelum: You're the one that should watch it.

Tom: What are you trying to say?

Lelum: *(Meaningfully)* I said you are the one that should watch it, not me.

Tom: It would help if you clarified.

Lelum: Would it? I know more about you than you think.

Paddy: *(Urgently)* Cut it out. *(To Sean)* You were saying Sean.

Sean: Our Irish virgins would never debase themselves. Our soldiers come from decent homes where the fear of God and love of Ireland go hand in hand.

Jack: Well let me tell you something Sean Trean. Your Irish boys and girls are no angels. Did you know Hanratty's mule died yesterday?

Sean: What has Hanratty's mule to do with it?

Sean: Did you hear Michael?

Michael: *(Absorbed with shovelling mixture into bucket)* I have no

time to be involved in argument just now. Carry on without
me. Nothing in this world, and I mean nothing, is going to
stay the building of this wall between here and nightfall.
*(Takes full bucket to shored boards and empties it therein.
Busies himself with trowel arranging it inside)*

Paddy: I heard about the mule. He collapsed going to the creamery
or something.

Jack: Or something is right. I'll tell you how he died. Until
recently that mule was a healthy five-year old without a
blemish, as fine an animal as was ever fathered by a stallion
ass. Yet suddenly he collapses. Mrs Hanratty suspected he
might be poisoned so she sent for Dick Savage the vet. Dick
Savage opened the mule's belly, right down the middle. *(To
Sean)* You know what he found?

Sean: How the devil do I know?

Jack: I'm asking you what Dick Savage the vet found in the
stomach of Hanratty's mule?

Sean: You tell me.

Jack: I'll tell you all right. He found one partly-digested, outsize
ladies' corset which no doubt once restrained the bulging
belly of one of your famous Irish virgins.

Sean: Rubbish.

Jack: Ask the vet. He found two brassieres also partly digested. He
found three ladies slips very well chewed, one of 'em em-
broidered. He found what looked like the remnants of eleven
silk stockings and a buckle from a woman's shoe. He found
the partial remains of eleven pairs of ladies' knickers, thor-
oughly ground up and all but digested and last but not least
twenty-seven pairs of ladies' home-made elastic garters.
Now are you convinced that your Irish soldier is no different
from any other soldier?

Lelum: If the knickers and the corsets were partly digested and
presumably on their way to being fully digested what was
the actual cause of death?

Paddy: I know. 'Twas the buckle.

Jack: No it wasn't. It was the garters. The mule was unable to digest the elastic.

Sean: I don't believe one word of it. Ladies' knickers indeed.

Jack: All you have to do is ask the vet if you don't believe me. What surprises me is that the unfortunate mule found knickers there at all because half those ones coming into town now never wore knickers in their lives.

Sean: *(Explodes)* These are heinous and unfounded allegations.

Jack: Half of them wouldn't know a pair of knickers from a pair of polo drawers.

Michael: *(Suddenly turning from his labours to Paddy and Tom)* In the name of God have you two not gone in yet?

Tom: We were just leaving.

Michael: Get out of it and get straight to your books the minute you've eaten.

Paddy: How's the wall going dada?

Michael: You might say it's at the critical stage. That's why I have to devote all my powers of concentration to it. For that reason I will repeat myself for the last time and ask the two of you to get indoors and have your supper.

Tom: It seems to me to be a bit crooked here, and look here, it seems to have sunk.

Michael: Those are small things, easily rectified. The main object is to get the thing built. It will be an easy matter to polish it up when it's finished. Now for the final time get in to your supper.

Tom: Just trying to offer a bit of helpful criticism.

Michael: *(Shouts)* I'll count to three and if the two of you have not gone indoors by that time ... one ...two...

(Exit Paddy and Tom)

Michael: It's easy to criticise. It's not easy to create.

Jack: We called to find out if you were coming for a gargle?

Michael: To tell you the truth boys I'm a bit low in the pocket. Payday is still a week to go.

Jack: Come on. I have enough for the three of us.

Michael: No thanks. That's not my way.

Lelum: Your word is good at Hogans.

Michael: I'm already up to my eyes at Hogans. Anyway, I've made up my mind that nothing is going to come between me and this wall, not for the next few days at any rate. You two go ahead ...

Jack: Fair enough so.

(Exit Jack and Sean)

Michael: *(Expected more persuasion. Turns to the wall and works for a while. Looks in the direction of Jack and Sean, then up at the scorching sun. About to exit after Sean and Jack)*

   The thirst will be gone by sundown. The wall'll still be there tomorrow!

(Enter Moses McCoy)

Moses: Good evening Master.

Michael: Good evening to you Moses.

Moses: Have you had any account from the war department, Master?

Michael: The letter came yesterday Moses. Hang on there a minute and I'll get it for you.

(Exit Michael. Moses examines the wall. Re-enter Michael)

Michael: *(Holding letter aloft)* Here it is Moses. *(He hands it to Moses who rips it open. He extracts cheque and flings envelope away)*

Moses: Thirty-one pounds seven shillings and threepence. This is the price paid by the wretch we call God for my two sons. Thirty-one pounds seven shillings and threepence. Hardly sixteen pounds apiece. Who says thank God now? What fool says God is good? God is no damned good, never was and never will be world without end ...

Michael: Now, now, Moses. Don't upset yourself. *(Places a hand on his shoulder)*

Moses: I'd like to give you a few pounds for your trouble Master.

Michael: You owe me nothing.

Moses: A drink then. We'll have a good drink.

Michael: You couldn't have asked me at a worse time, I'm up to my neck in this wall.

Moses: Don't renege on me Master. There's enough reneged on me.

Michael: Well I'll have one then.

Moses: If you'll have one you'll have two. We'll have a night of it. No one pays but me. Come on now. I won't hear of no ... *(He leads Michael off)*

(The light fades to night-time. Tom enters stealthily and begins to tune the radio. Presently Lily enters in her night-clothes and cardigan)

Lily: Master Tom, what are you doing up at this hour?

Tom: I heard tell that Haw-Haw was doing a late night broadcast, but I can't tune this blasted thing. Reception on medium is fair but BBC 376 is swamping the signal. If you go for 391, BBC Toulouse squeeze Bremen and Hamburg off the air.

Lily: That's desperate.

Tom: If we had a more powerful set I'd try Bremen on long.

Lily: Try it on medium 500.

(Tom looks at her in wonderment. Turns the dial to 500 and we immediately hear Haw-Haw)

Haw-Haw: What was England's contribution? An expeditionary force which carried out a glorious retreat, leaving all its equipment and arms behind, a force whose survivors arrived back in Britain, as *The Times* admits, practically naked. No doubt the soldiers fled according to orders; no doubt they found themselves utterly at a loss to cope with German dive bombers and other engines of modern scientific warfare. But whatever excuses may be found for their plight, the solid fact remains that the men who made the war were reduced to boasting of a precipitous and disastrous retreat as the most glorious achievement in history. Such a claim could only besmirch the proud regimental standards inscribed with the real victories of two centuries. What the politicians regarded, or professed to regard, as a triumph, the soldiers regarded as a bloody defeat from which they were extremely fortunate to escape alive ... The glorious R.A.F. was too busy dropping bombs on fields and graveyards in Germany to have any time available for the battle of France.

Tom: How did you know that, Lily?

Lily: I heard the lads below in Hanratty's sayin' that was the way to get yer man Haw-Haw.

Tom: *(Hangdog)* You know I'm banned from going to Hanratty's Lily.

Lily: I know. Sure Sadie Coffey is very lonesome after you.

Tom: *(Bitterly)* Sadie Coffey won't stay lonesome very long. *(Pause. Passionately)* I'm starved for a good coort Lily.

Lily: Turn that oul thing off. Is there no music in that wireless?

(Tom turns the knob. We lose Haw-Haw and pick up Marlene Dietrich singing 'Lily Marlene')

Tom: Dance Lily?

Lily: Don't be an eejit. I'm going for a piddle.

(She disappears into the outside lavatory. Tom dejected. After a moment)

Master Tom, I'm having trouble locking the door after me in the dark. Will you give me a hand.

(Tom looks to the audience with a wide grin and goes to the lavatory and closes the door behind him)

(Curtain)

ACT TWO

Scene II

Action as before. The time is three weeks later. It is well into July. A fine starry night. Michael Barnett is busily re-arranging cement and gravel mixture within shored boards. The wall has reached the halfway stage. At one side Moses McCoy uses a shovel to mix cement and gravel. From time to time he adds a little water.

Moses: How long now since you started it Master?

Michael: Let me see. *(Cogitates)* It must be five or six weeks all told. God knows I suppose it could be the six weeks. Of course I could do nothing for the past fortnight between the rain and storm.

Moses: That's the truth. Only for the break in the weather you'd have it finished by now. There's no sane man would deny that.

Michael: Still you'll have to admit that the critical stage is past. It should be all plain sailing from now on. Let's have a drop of porter before we proceed any further.

(He goes to the table and pours from enamel bucket into glasses)

Moses: I see your soldier son at home Master.

Michael: He is. He is. He got a week's leave. Unfortunately he goes back tomorrow.

Moses: He's a fine man for his years.

Michael: He's all that. Isn't he a grand sight in the uniform?

Moses: Oh without doubt.

Michael: Of course I had an uncle as fine a man as ever broke bread. In fact my father and grandfather were exceptional fellows. They had a great natural strength.

Moses: You're no bad man yourself Master.

Michael: One time Moses. One time.

Moses: I had great sons Master. The two of them were well over the six feet and as broad as that wall you're building. The strength of them would frighten you ... and to be carried away by that hobo that scoffs at us all above in his heaven.

(Produces bottle of methylated spirits with which he laces porter. He proffers bottle to Michael who recoils)

Michael: You'll face God quicker than you think if you keep drinking that stuff. Why don't you drink whiskey itself?

Moses: My money is all gone Master.

Michael: Considering everything it made a fair battle. Good health to you Moses. *(He quaffs from his glass)*

Moses: I notice Master you seldom drink spirits of any kind.

Michael: It's not by choice I assure you. It agrees neither with my constitution nor my pocket. There are times when I become ravenous for it. I love whiskey. I love the gurgle of it in the snout of a bottle and I love the rich plop of it when it falls into a glass. I love the way it babbles and bubbles when a bottle is shaken. As for the taste of it I find it goes beyond words. That first drop of it hits the walls of the chest a ferocious rattle but after that it lights up the interior and there is a wonderful lunacy in the head. Ah Moses there were few born with the natural love of whiskey that was granted to me.

(Enter Mary Barnett. She is followed by Lily)

Mary: I want to speak to you Michael. Something very serious has happened.

Michael: Yes Mary. What is it?

Mary: I'm afraid it's private Michael.

Michael: Well I can't right away. It's a dry night and that heap of cement mix over there is likely to get hard unless I use it up at once.

Mary: It's important.

Michael: I know. I won't be long dear.

Mary: I have a few things to do. I won't press you now. I'll be back in ten minutes and I want nobody here but members of our own family. Come along Lily.

(Exit Mary Barnett followed by Lily. Michael stands puzzled, wondering)

Moses: I'll go.

Michael: No. She didn't mean it like that.

Moses: She's like a woman who would have enough of out-siders in the place for a while.

Michael: You think so?

Moses: I call on many a house Master and I can tell a woman's moods. She seems a very agitated woman. I have the feeling I should start evacuating. Women are like the ocean, peaceful and calm one minute and the next violent and raging. That woman is simmering with a bit. I'd say she's near the boil. I'll be on my way. *(Makes to exit)*

Michael: What was your own wife like, Moses?

Moses: *(Stops and turns)* My wife, Master, was a beauty. I often wished she was eighty years of age so I wouldn't be jealous of her anymore. *(Points upwards)* You see all them stars ... all them together wasn't as bright as her smile. Her hair was red but sometimes when the wind played on it 'twould turn to russet or if 'twas caught in the light of the sun 'twould take a hundred shades, one of 'em brighter than the next. Oh Jesus Master 'twas an awful sweeping. If I had God now I'd break him in two. I'll face him soon though and then he'll have nowhere to hide from me ... so long Master.

Michael: So long Moses.

(Moses exits with a sigh. Michael returns to the wall)

(Enter Jack strong and Sean Trean. They wear their armbands)

Sean: *(To Jack)* And I say to you that Ireland divided will never be at peace.

Michael: *(Noticing Sean Trean and Jack Strong for the first time)* Ah gentlemen ... what do you two think now?

Jack: *(Ignoring Sean)* You've really made progress. I can't believe it.

Sean: There's no doubt but you've passed the critical stage.

Jack: If the weather holds and it looks like it will it wouldn't surprise me if the wall wasn't standing on it's own two feet by the end of July.

Michael: Can you imagine it in the autumn covered with lichens and draped with red ivy. Picture it in your mind. The wind rustles through the ivy and a flight of starlings suddenly erupts from the depths with a whirring of tiny wings. Or picture it in the moonlight when the beams of silver fall on the ivy leaves. What a romantic place this back garden will be when that time comes.

(Sean Trean examines the enamel bucket)

Michael: I agree with you but I am not going to make the fatal mistake of setting myself a time limit. I am not going to be rushed. That could mean mistakes and I can't afford to make one at this stage. *(Steps back and surveys his work)*

(Sean Trean examines the enamel bucket)

I'm afraid it's empty Sean. Building is dry work.

Sean: We had a notion of going to Hogans for a few.

Michael:	Don't let me stop you.
Jack:	Aren't you coming?
Michael:	How can I? Conditions are ideal for building and anyway the missus wants a word with me. Maybe later.

(Enter Lelum followed by Paddy and Tom. Tom would seem to have a black eye. He carries togs and football boots and jersey wrapped up in a bundle. Paddy wears togs, stockings and football boots. He carries his clothes in an untidy bundle)

Sean:	Who won the match?
Lelum:	'Twas never finished. The bloody crowd rushed the pitch.
Michael:	*(Advances)* Were the three of you stuck in the row?
Lelum:	We were lucky we weren't kicked to death. We ran for it.
Michael:	*(To Tom)* What happened to you?
Tom:	I ran into somebody's fist.
Jack:	The word becomes flesh.
Tom:	Sorry Jack?
Jack:	Your football epic, son. Give us a blast of it.
Tom:	Right so

(Tom starts slowly and builds up to an almost unbearable climax, egged on by all save Michael)

The teams fared forth and the backs went back
Then the heavens opened with a mighty crack
And there stood Mars with a face as black
As a thousand years of sorrow,
It wasn't Beelzebub's blighted blast
Or a sombre, lumbering cloud that passed
A rogue from the west where the pack was massed

For to drown the green fields on the morrow.

It was not the tension that rose from the crowd
Heads yet unblooded and spirits uncowed
That blackened the sun with its ominous shroud
With its shadows and dark shades legion
It was not an intense flight or stare
Assembled that moment from everywhere
That suddenly sullied the summer air
That settled like night on the region.

No, no for damsels devoted to prayer
Attested Mars trod on the trembling air
It was none but the glorious God of war
As he prized the heavens asunder.
Then he raised his hands than the welkin higher
His nostrils blowing and billowing fire
As his words rolled over the land entire
Like the terrific tones of thunder.
'Harken!' roared he 'to the words I say
Let the lines be drawn for the coming fray
Let there be no quarter this glorious day
Let each wound another nourish.
Let the blows fall fast. Let the blood flow free
Let the groin know elbow, boot and knee.
Let knuckles white set the molars free
Let the warrior spirit flourish.

'Let Mack strike Mooney and Mooney Mack.
Let Stack strike Looney and Looney Stack.
Let Fitz flake Flynn and let Flynn flake back
With the knee and the nail and the knuckle.
Let Kane strike Cooney and Cooney Kane
Let Kane strike Lally and Lally Lane
Let Maine strike Mooney and Mooney Maine.
With the belt and the boot and the buckle.'

Michael: *(To Tom and Paddy)* That's enough of that. Get inside and change and come right back here for further instructions.

Tom: There's a dance on tonight. The exam is over.

Michael: I said report back here for instructions.

Tom: *(Saluting stiffly)* Yes sir.

                    (Exit Tom and Paddy)

Michael: Where's Tony?

Lelum: He's bringing on the girls.

Michael: Who started the fight?

Lelum: Somebody booed a decision by the referee and the crowd ran on to the field.

Jack: That would never happen in rugby. There's no discipline in Gaelic football. A young lad could be maimed and he could whistle for justice.

Sean: You never liked our native games.

Jack: That's not so. What I'm saying is that there isn't enough discipline.

Sean: And what I'm saying is that any Irishman who plays rugby is a swine.

Jack: Will you listen to that!

Sean: And any Irishman who watches the game of rugby is a bigger swine. He is a low-down, dirty, stinking sewer rat. You can take your British garrison games and you can stick them up in the highest rafter of you know where.

Jack: What chance has this country when we have mentalities like this? There will never be an end to stupidity.

Sean: There will never be an end to the Gaelic tradition, to the ideal that Ireland is the proudest nation in Europe, the oldest nation in Europe and according to the pope the most Catholic country of all. I'll spell it out once more. Any Irishman who plays soccer, rugby or cricket is a dirty renegade.

Michael: What about pitch and toss?

Sean: It's not as bad as the games I've mentioned.

Jack: What about Ju Jitsu?

Michael: And Russian roulette?

Sean: Mocking is catching.

Michael: And it's not going to get this wall built. *(Enter Tony Barnett, the oldest son. He is dressed in the uniform of the Irish army. He wears a field cap and the landyard of the artillery)*

Sean: Ah Tony ... and how are you enjoying your holiday? *(Places his arm around Tony's shoulder)*

Tony: Great entirely Sean.

Jack: What was the match like?

Tony: It was all right till the spectators joined in.

Jack: Ah yes. The great Gaels of Ireland.

Sean: *(To Jack)* Can you think of nothing good to say about your native land?

Jack: I can but it wouldn't be good enough for you. *(To Tony)* So you're away tomorrow.

Tony: Yes Jack. I'll have to be in the barracks at ten o'clock tomorrow night.

Sean: Duty first. When duty calls a soldier must obey.

        (Enter Paddy and Tom. They wear armbands. They are followed by Lelum)

Tom: Reporting for further instructions.

Tony: I see you're all in the local defence force.

Sean: Now that we have a professional soldier in our midst why shouldn't we let him put us through our paces. *(All gather* *round Tony eagerly)*

Tony: I'm not a drill Master. I'm just a private soldier who's never given an order in his life.

Michael: You're a trained soldier and that's all that matters. Come on lads. Get your weapons.

(They all make haste to find whatever mock rifles they can. Lelum and Michael use shovels, Sean Trean uses a sledge. Others locate convenient pieces of timber)

Tony: Ah come off it. I'm no use at this kind of jazz.

Michael: You'll do. You're good enough for us.

Sean: This is a great moment for the town of Lolinn. Imagine to be drilled by a man I knew as a child. A man I helped to rear.

Michael: Line up there now. We want no farcing. This has to be serious. Let's find out how good we are.

Sean: It may not be much in the eyes of the outside world but for us this is a highly historical occasion. *(They make an uneven line across the stage)*

Jack: *(To Lelum)* What a pity we haven't a camera. The world shouldn't be deprived of a sight like this.

(When they are lined up they await instructions eagerly. They hold their rifles at various angles, all different)

Michael: We're waiting Tony.

Tony: Oh, well – gasra aire.

(They all come to attention)

Ardig arum.

(They shoulder arms. Business – Sean puts 'rifle' on wrong shoulder. Jack takes pleasure in correcting him)

Déanaighe dhá líne.

(They form a double line)

Clé casaigh

(They turn to left, except Sean)

Sean: *(Aside to Jack)* In the name a' Jazus what's 'cosseagae'?

Jack: Left turn!

Sean: *(Turns)* Oh!

Tony: Go mear máirséal.

(All march off whistling)

(Alone on stage Tony shakes his head with a smile. He goes to wall and examines latest developments there. Off can be heard the distant sound of whistling. The volume increases and the company enters whistling the 'Boys of Wexford' or the likes. They march across stage and exit at the other side. While they are off Mary Barnett enters)

Mary: *(Shakes her head)* God help us all. They've no more sense than children.

Tony: *(Immediately concerned by her air of worry)* What's the matter mother?

Mary: Does it show that much Tony?

Tony: You look down and out. Is anything wrong?

Mary: There's a lot wrong Tony.

Tony: Can you tell me?

Mary: I wouldn't know where to begin. Wait 'till your father and the boys come back and the rest have gone. There's a lot to be said. It's not for outsiders to hear. This can only be resolved by ourselves. I could cry my eyes out this minute if it would do any good.

Tony: Ah come on now mother. It can't be that bad.

Mary: It's bad enough Tony. Tony I want you to tell me something.

Tony: If I can.

Mary: About girls Tony.

Tony: What about them?

Mary: Do you respect them?

Tony: Yes ... of course.

Mary: You go out with girls a lot?

Tony: Some weekends yes.

Mary: Are you going steady?

Tony: Oh mother, on twenty-one shillings a week?

Mary: But do you have a regular girl?

Tony: Why don't you tell me what you really want to know and I'll do my best to answer?

Mary: All right. Do you respect all the girls you go with?

Tony: I don't fully understand you.

Mary: I just want to know if you behave yourselves with girls?

Tony: I don't know how to answer that one. I don't know exactly what you mean by behave.

Mary: You kiss girls.

Tony: Of course.

Mary: Do you go beyond that?

Tony: I don't know what you're driving at.

Mary: Oh don't be so evasive Tony. Will you please tell me if you've ever been familiar with a girl?

Tony: *(Seeking an avenue to escape)* Familiar ... what's that supposed to mean?

Mary: Jesus Tony have you ever been intimate with a girl?

Tony: Look mother I don't know what to say to you. I love you and respect you and I don't want to disillusion you. The army is a hard school. There are different codes. I go out with girls because I'm lonely.

Mary: Thank you Tony. I think you've answered my question.

Tony: Of course I've been intimate with women. There's a world war going on around us and I'm a soldier. I have never wronged a girl or I've never misled an innocent girl. I know I've done terrible wrong by your standards but by my own I'm not so bad. What's happened to me has happened to every mother's son. I want you to know mother that I respect girls whether they expect it or not. Don't be angry with me.

Mary: I'm not. It's just that I took certain things for granted. I'm hurt and I'm disappointed but I'm not angry with you Tony. Understand that.

Tony: Yes mother.

Mary: I keep forgetting you're not my baby anymore, that you're a man of the world, that you have to be what you are.

(Tony turns his head aside. She would go to him to console him but she hesitates. Then from a distance can be heard the beat of a drum and whistling. The volume increases. Enter the company. At the rear Paddy beats on a toy drum, it is ancient and battered but effective, nonetheless. The company is deadly serious and intent on presenting a military appearance. They pass by and exit but not before Mary Barnett seizes Tom and pulls him aside. The others ignore everything. Exit the company)

Tom: *(Airily)* I was enjoying it. What's the matter anyway?

Mary: Don't you know?

Tom: Know what?

Mary: About Lily?

Tom: What about Lily?

Mary: I'm deadly serious Tom so don't play about with me. You mean you don't know what's the matter with Lily?

Tom: Cross my heart I don't know what you're talking about. Honestly mother I don't. *(Turns to Tony)* What is it anyway? What's all this jazz about Lily.

Tony: I don't know.

Mary: I'm weak with worry that's on top of me this day. Tom had you anything to do with Lily since she came to work for us?

Tom: What are you on about?

Mary: Answer the question.

Tom: I would if I knew what you meant.

(Mary suddenly snatches stick from his hand and lets him have it heavily across the body)

Tom: *(Jumps backward)* Hey look out, that hurts.

Mary: You don't know what hurt is Tom. Poor Lily O'Dea knows what hurt is. Poor innocent Lily O'Dea that I thought was safe under my roof.

Tom: *(Not convincing. To Tony)* Somebody tell me what it's all about.

Mary: You know what it's all about.

Tom: But I don't.

Mary: Don't you know she's going to have a baby?

Tom: What?

Mary: A baby. You know what a baby is?

Tom: Yes. I do.

Mary: Well Lily is going to have one of them. Come nearer to me Tom. *(He draws near to her)* Do you know anything about this baby?

Tom: What would I know?

              (Suddenly Mary unleashes a vicious swipe with stick and catches him fairly with it. He covers his head with his hands but makes no attempt to evade the second swipe)

Mary: *(Loudly)* What would you know Tom? Is that what you say ... you're a hard one Tom, a hard man. I never dreamed I would rear a son like you. *(She strikes him viciously across the legs)* Now will you tell me about Lily O'Dea?

Tom: It was only once. I swear it was only once. They were all doing it to her, all the lads.

Mary: No they weren't. Lelum wasn't and Paddy wasn't. You were the one. The poor girl was in our charge, in our care. She was entrusted to us. What in the name of Mary am I going to tell her mother? What am I going to say to her? How am I going to begin. A son of mine is the father of the bastard your daughter is going to have. My son Tom is the man.

Tom: Mother, mother listen to me. It's not true. She had soldiers long before me. She had other fellows, farmers boys and clerks long before me. I swear that to you mother. I'm not responsible.

Mary: Will you listen to him.

Tom: *(Advancing with his hands outstretched)* As true as God mother!

Mary: The poor fooleen of a girl. She named them all, all the
          soldiers, all the others. She didn't name you Tom. She
          wouldn't tell me about you because you were of the house.
          Innocent as she is she knew what you did was the worst.
          You betrayed a trust. You cheated on your upbringing and
          the faith she had in you. I had to ask her. I had to be sure. I
          wouldn't be a good mother if I didn't make certain. *(Tony
          advances towards her but she wards him off)*

Tony: Mother you're being too hard on yourself.

Mary: I had to be satisfied. Were there any others, I asked. She
          didn't answer. Tell me the truth Lily I said. She still
          wouldn't answer me. Was Tom one of them I asked. No
          answer. Was Tom one of them I asked again. This time she
          nodded her head and she cried her eyes out.

Tom: It was only a few weeks ago I was with her. I had nothing to
          do with the child. That happened long before.

Mary: Maybe so but what matters is that you took advantage of her
          and which is worse you did it under this roof. I never
          thought I'd live to see the day that a son of mine would
          dishonour an innocent. You ... *(She beats him relentlessly
          across the garden)* You vile and wretched thing. At this
          moment I wouldn't care if I never saw you again in my life
          ... *(He falls in a heap at one side. Tony helps Tom to his feet
          and thence to a chair. He sits hangdog. In the distance can
          be heard the whistling and the drum. This time it is 'It's a
          long way to Tipperary')*

Mary: Will they ever grow up?

Tony: They're happy and at least that's something.

Mary: You haven't had much of a holiday Tony. I'm sorry but I
          wouldn't be much of a mother to either one of you if I
          closed my eyes to reality. I was tempted to do it, tempted to
          pretend that Tom was innocent.

          (The whistling and drumming grows louder)

          Bring them to a halt this time Tony like a good boy.

Tony: Whatever you say.

(Enter the company, as game and as martial as ever, proudly singing along, heads held high, whistling their hearts out)

Tony: Greadáigh fúibh.

(They mark time)

Gasra stad.

(They halt)

Clé casaíg.

(They turn left)

Gaonáig airm.

(They bring arms to side)

Seasaí araís
(They stand at ease)

Gasra scaipíg.

(They dismiss)

Michael: As fine a body of men begob as you'd find anywhere.

Sean: True for you. What do you think Tony?

Tony: There's no doubt but you're as good as any I've seen.

Sean: We're ready and we're waiting. We won't be found wanting when the hour comes.

Jack: What hour?

Sean: The hour our country needs us.

Jack: The day the country depends on the likes of us that's curtains for the country.

Michael: Now, now. Don't be too sure. *(He immediately proceeds to where mixture is and commences to mix with shovel)* Remember Thermopylae? They were only a handful.

Mary: I'd like a talk with you Michael.

Michael: Very well ... *(To Sean and Jack)* I think I'll go to Hogans with you after all. I could do with a few pints. God knows it's been a long day. Hang on there just awhile lads 'till I listen to my long suffering wife. Now Mary girl what is it?

Mary: It's for the family.

Michael: You know Sean and Jack. There's no need for ...

Mary: Listen to me Michael and get it through your head. I don't want Jack and Sean to hear what I have to say.

Jack: We were just going anyway.

Michael: It must be something terrible altogether ... *(Jack and Sean hang on although they have edged towards exit)*

Mary: In the name of God will you tell them to go. What do you want them for anyway? What good are they to you?

Michael: Mary ... Mary. These are my friends. *(Appalled at her forthrightness)* You mustn't ...

Mary: You wouldn't know what a friend is if you had one. We're your friends, your family. What do you want these for, to hide behind is it? Whenever there's anything serious to be discussed you hang on to them like a drowning man. Why do you need them so much? Is it because reality proves too much for you?

Michael: I must say I resent this ... I won't forget it in a hurry.

Mary: *(Scorn)* You resent ... Look at them still hanging around. Wouldn't you think they'd know better and allow us our privacy.

Michael: What's the matter with you? Why do you talk like this?

Mary: Because it's true. *(Points to Sean and Jack)* You concern yourself with these and with your wall instead of us your family.

Michael: Dammit I'm always with you.

Mary: You're here all right but you're not with us.

Michael: You disgrace me in front of my friends.

Mary: If they were your friends they would have slipped away quietly ages ago and left us to ourselves.

(Suddenly turns furious on Jack and Sean and screams)

Will you get to Christ out of here and leave us to ourselves. Go on. Get out. Damn you, get out …

(Jack and Sean exit hastily)

Michael: They'll never come here again. Why do you seek to humiliate me so much? Do you get pleasure from it? Those were my friends.

Mary: Those were the blinds you drew down in front of your eyes when you didn't want to see. Those were the barriers you kept between yourself and your true obligations.

Michael: I don't know what you mean.

Mary: Of course you still have your wall but that's not enough in itself.

Michael: Don't you think it's time you told me what this is all about.

Mary: That's more of it. Why should I have to tell you? You should know yourself.

Michael: I'm not omniscient.

Mary: Our serving girl is pregnant. That will do to start with.

Lelum: Oh God no!

Michael: Lily?

Mary: Yes Lily.

Michael: Do you know who's responsible?

Mary: I'm afraid there was more than one.

Michael: The little fool. Soldiers I suppose?

Mary: Yes.

Michael: Another war casualty.

Mary: Your son Tom was involved in it too. He must take his share of the blame.

Michael: *(To Tom) (Furiously)* Christ I've a mind to maim you. How could you? Look at me between the eyes when I speak to you. Lift up your head. It's true is it? ... What your mother says. *(Tom nods)* Speak.

Tom: Yes.

Michael: You broke your promise to me. You have no honour, no word. You're left without a decent attribute.

Mary: You're as much to blame as he is.

Michael: How in the name of God can you say that?

Mary: Long ago he should have been horse-whipped. The time of Hanratty's shed he should have been beaten within an inch of his life. Instead you left it up to me and I'm not able for it. He wears me out. I'm weary from him.

Michael: Well he won't get away with it this time. *(Looks for something with which to beat him)*

Mary: Jesus that's you all over. Closing the stable door when the horse is gone. What good is it beating him now? What worse can he do? He can sink no lower. You're wasting your time.

Michael: *(To Tom)* Get up.

(Tom rises slowly)

Have you anything to say?

(Tom shakes his head)

You can go now, not to bed. You can go where you like and I don't care what time you come back. I refuse to be concerned about you. Go on.

(Tom goes towards exit despondently)

Go where you like and come when you like. You're your own boss from now on.

(Silently Tom exits)

Tony: I don't know what good that's going to do.

Lelum: What's past is past. He's no angel but which of us is.

Mary: You tell that to Lily's mother and father.

Lelum: I know. I know but sending him off isn't going to make Lily any the less pregnant and that's what you've done, sent him off. He might not come back.

Michael: He'll come back.

Paddy: I'll bet he won't.

Michael: And pray who the hell asked you for an opinion?

Paddy: I'm accused of no crime yet.

Michael: There's bloody rebellion fermenting here. You watch what you say. I'll not take a word of guff from anyone here. I feel like a drink. In fact I feel like going on one hell of a booze.

Mary: You'd better not. There's a lot more to be set to rights before you do anything.

Tony: What a night this is turning out to be.

Mary: I'm sorry Tony. I know it's your last night but it's better this way, better for all of us and better for the future. Let's all get our piece said. What about Lelum?

Michael: I told you all about that.

Mary: You told me nothing. You made a half promise which could mean anything.

Michael: *(To Lelum)* All right. I should be able to manage to send you to university this coming October.

Lelum: I don't want to go.

Michael: It will be a sacrifice but I think I can manage it.

Lelum: Other fathers with less seem to be better off. Managing seems to be no problem to them.

Michael: That's because they never smoked a cigarette or never took a damned drink in their lives or never went anywhere or never ate half enough. By Christ they wouldn't buy a blasted newspaper some of them!

Mary: Their families benefited if they didn't and that's what matters.

Michael: *(To Lelum)* Look. I told you I might manage it. I thought you'd say thanks at least.

Lelum: Thanks ... but I don't want to go.

Michael: You'll go where you're told.

Lelum: Come off it. You're not dealing with your school children now. I have no notion of going back to school books again. I've been too long away.

Tony: It's hard when you're too long away. It's next to impossible to go back.

Michael: Listen to who's talking. How can you speak about school books? You with your fine education and your experience in the civil service and all you managed to make out of yourself was a private soldier.

Tony: There's nothing wrong with being a private soldier.

Michael: I have nothing against private soldiers and well you know it. What I'm saying is that you could have become an officer or a non com at least.

Tony: I don't want to be an officer.

Michael: You might have thought of your parents and your family, the pleasure it would have brought us to see you with a commission.

Paddy: The pleasure it would have brought you? What about the pleasure being a private brings to him.

Michael: One more word and I'll boot you so hard in the posterior your front teeth will fall out. *(To Tony)* You could have been an officer no trouble at all.

Tony: I told you I didn't want to be.

Michael: But why didn't you want to be? What's the point in having an education if you won't use it?

Tony: Being an officer isn't everything.

Michael: I didn't say it was. What I'm trying to say is that by not taking a commission you shirked. It was easier and more fashionable to become a private.

Tony: Why didn't I spend my leave in barracks with all the other misfits?

Mary: Because you're a good boy at heart and you wanted to be home with your own. That was natural but it wasn't natural for you to be a private soldier.

Lelum: *(To parents)* You two want an army with nothing but officers.

Michael: No. The truth is that you dodged out Tony. You refused to face up to your responsibilities.

Lelum: *(Carefully repeating)* Refusal to face up to his responsibilities ... I wonder now where he got that from.

Michael: You're just as bad. Now that you have the chance to go to the university you back down. You probably wanted never to go in the first place. What's going to become of you? What are you going to do with yourself?

Lelum: I'm going to be an actor.

(Michael raises his head quizzically)

Michael: You're going to be what?

Lelum: An actor.

Michael: Is this a deliberate attempt to ridicule me?

Lelum: It's not. I'm serious. I auditioned for Mr McMaster last week and I got this letter back yesterday. 'Dear Lelum, thank you for reading for us in Ballybunion last week, and also for helping with the raffle in the hall each night, much appreciated. Your audition piece was well-phrased, and you have an agreeable stage presence. Mind you, if you were to join us for a tour you would have to set your sights a little lower: I'll be reviving *Romeo and Juliet* next spring and will as usual be playing that particular young man myself – but there might be Benvolio, or the County Paris, excellent parts for beginners, to speak nothing of crowd. Do drop me a line a little before Christmas and I'll let you know what the situation holds for you then. My address is Baily Cottage, Howth, Co. Dublin. Yours sincerely, Anew McMaster'.

Michael: What crime so monstrous have I unwittingly committed that I should be visited with this revelation from one of my own flesh and blood? Be anything. Be a spy, an informer, even a pimp or a whoremaster. Dammit and blast it be a hangman but don't be an actor.

Lelum:　That's what I am going to be.

Michael:　No man in his right mind would be an actor.

Lelum:　That's because you can't act yourself.

Michael:　Can't I? I can act a damned sight better than many of your so-called professional actors but unfortunately I cannot afford to. I have to preserve my acting talent for my daily survival. I have none to spare for the theatre. I find that I have to act from morning till night in this house, if I am to hold on to my sanity. If I gave vent to my real feelings skin and hair would fly from one end of the day to the other.

Mary:　I wish to God you would.

Michael:　Look … enough of this nonsense. Have we nothing better to do than stand around here arguing? *(He locates trowel)* I have to spread this plaster before it hardens. Then I'm going to have a long drink.

Lelum:　I'll be leaving in the morning.

Michael:　Why must you do this to me?

Mary:　He's doing nothing to you.

Michael:　Leave us alone. *(To Lelum)* Is it deliberate? Is it your revenge for the times I've failed you? God knows I must have failed you all from time to time. I'm not a god. I'm human and I make mistakes. But each one of you would have me a failure. I'm not a failure. I have done all the things I wanted to do. I married the woman I loved. I raised intelligent sons. I suppose they had to be human too. I don't expect them to be perfect. Why then should I be expected to be perfect?

Mary:　We don't expect you to be perfect and you know that well. Have I ever asked perfection of you?

Michael: No ... but my sons have and still do.

Mary: You wrong them. All they seek is fair play.

Michael: Whose side are you on anyway? I'm doing my best. You've been cribbing and nagging now for weeks on end, from the first moment in fact that I started to build this wall. Secretly you're all scoffing at it. I've seen you smirk, all of you.

Paddy: I didn't mean it.

Michael: Maybe not but you belittled it all the same.

Paddy: I didn't.

Michael: Oh yes you did. I'm not as blind as you all think I am. This wall is not a luxury. It's a necessity. I make no apologies for building it. To tell the truth though I'm sorry I ever started it. It's brought nothing but misery. *(To Lelum)* So you want to be an actor and you're determined.

Lelum: Yes.

Michael: And I don't want you to be one. However I won't stand in your way. An actor. I'll give you what I can before you leave.

Lelum: Thanks.

Mary: Let's go in. There's a chill coming on.

Michael: *(To Tony)* And you Tony? Will you make an effort when you go back? You could be an officer in three months.

Tony: All my friends are private soldiers. I wouldn't be happy as anything else.

Michael: You'll all end up failures.

Tony: It's what I want ... like acting is what Lelum wants.

Paddy: And like poetry is what I want ...

Michael: Shut up and fetch Tom.

(Exit Paddy)

Mary: You can't blame them for being what they want to be. It's your own fault. You were never stern. You have no right to crib if they're the same as you. It was you who made them what they are.

Michael: I'm to blame for everything am I?

Mary: I didn't mean it like that.

Michael: Then you had no right to say so. I'm confused enough by you as it is.

Mary: Wouldn't you tell the truth for once and admit you're creating your own confusion.

Michael: Tell the truth for once? You're telling me now I've never told the truth in my life.

Mary: You're twisting my words.

Michael: I am not. You're the one who's prolonging this argument. Damn you you're never wrong. It's always me. You should be christened Mary-never-wrong because according to yourself you're always right.

Mary: Will you be straight you hypocrite? Will you have the guts to take the blame just this once? You are to blame for what your sons are, not me. Jesus what am I but a glorified skiv. I have no money. I go nowhere. I cook and I wash and I scrub. That's my function. I placed my trust in you to see that these boys of ours would be steered on the right course, but you closed your eyes when the storms came up.

Michael: The boys are all right.

Mary: They are not. You've done nothing for them, absolutely nothing. Every time a small sacrifice was needed you went out and you got drunk, or you turned your attention to something else, like the book you never finished or this wall you're at now. God you were an awful man for dodging.

Michael: Now that's a terrible exaggeration. It's a wonder you stuck it so long if I was so awful.

Mary: I had to stick it for my children's sake. There were times when I would have gone but I could not leave them. It was no fun listening to your drunken promises over the years and your hopeless plans that never came to anything. I believed you at first but after the children started to come I realised I was stuck with a man who would never move out of fairy-land.

Michael: You kept this in a long time.

Mary: It was never too far in. I had to think of the children but the children are men now and it's time it came out. I didn't want them like you. I don't want them making some girl foolish promises that they'll never be able to keep. I don't want them telling lies all their lives. You lied, lied, lied all the way through. Everything was going to be all right. You would turn over a new leaf and set everything to rights. I used believe you but Jesus, Mary and Joseph you turned over a thousand leaves Michael. I don't want them to live a lie, a dirty black lie that makes a mockery of love.

Michael: Not opposite the boys, please – you can't mean all this. You don't know what you're saying. This isn't like you. You're shocked by what Tom did.

Mary: Maybe, but if I am it's making me say what I've wanted to say for years.

Paddy: *(Enters)* He'll be along in a minute.

Mary: I started out our life in love with you but it died slowly, slowly, slowly, day after day, month after month, year after year. It died under your very eyes and you saw it die. You watched it die and you were content to do nothing about it. You dodged the reality of it like you dodged everything.

Michael: You can't mean all this. If I was so awful why bother with me at all?

Mary: Some women wouldn't. They give up the fight, not because they're tired or fed up but because they just can't be bothered. It's not worth it.

Michael: Tell me this? If as you say the love went after so many years what did we experience before the other children were born. Were we animals or what?

Mary: That's a rotten question.

Michael: You can't answer it.

Mary: I can but it's not fair, not here and now.

Michael: Tell me the truth.

Mary: I was a dutiful wife. I made a promise when I got married. I didn't go back on it.

Michael: But was it love what we had or was it purely animal!? That's what I want to know. It was only a travesty if there was no love.

Mary: A thing becomes a habit and a person doesn't know what it is. *(Screams at him)* Look, you don't start giving out to me, you that failed on every job you ever tried to do. I never failed you remember that. There was no escape for me. You had the pub and you had your fantasies and you had me silent, obedient and dutiful.

Michael: Does this mean that you haven't cared over the years, that you don't care now? It's incredible. Incredible. *(Turns away, pondering, perturbed)*

Mary: I care all right. Otherwise why would I be tearing myself apart now making a show of myself opposite my children. For all the good 'twill do I'm sure. That's the greatest curse, knowing it will do no good.

Paddy: He knows now. He really does. I know him.

Mary: No. It's a waste.

Paddy: You had to do it this way. Oh he knows. I know he does. I know by his face. Here's Tom.

(Enter Tom)

Mary: *(To Michael)* Let's hear you now. For God's sake do something sensible for a change.

Michael: *(To Tom)* Have you any sorrow in you for what you've done?

(Tom nods)

I'll give you a letter to a past pupil of mine in Manchester. He'll fix you up with a job for the present. You can't stay around here after what you've done. Some time, some distant time you can come back when the whole thing is another sorry episode in the history of local humanity. Come here.

(Tom comes near)

I don't find it easy to tell you go. I'll miss you more than I can say. This time, for the first time I have to be firm and I can tell you it hurts. I'm not condemning you. None of us are saints least of all me. Like Lelum's acting ... I too have sat with a holy face in the moonlight when seduction was the highest thought in my head.

Mary: But you didn't go further.

Michael: That may be so but it's all chance. Try to be a good boy in England Tom and when it's time for you to come home I'll send for you and everything will be all right again please God. Make it up with your mother.

(Hesitantly he faces Mary. He takes a step towards her weighing his chances. She extends her arms and he goes to her)

There's only one other job to do now before I go to bed. Fetch me the sledge.

(Paddy locates it and hands it to him)

Paddy: *(Alarmed)* What do you mean to do?

Michael: That wall.

Paddy: You can't.

Tony: We won't let you. Mother speak to him. Tell him we want the wall to stay.

Mary: What's the matter Michael? What are you doing to yourself?

Michael: Everybody stand back please.

(He flexes his shoulders and arms and lifts the sledge)

(All stand in path of his vent)

It was a dream anyway. I knew in my heart that fate would never let me finish it. This was inevitable. There's no other possible course open to me.

Paddy: We won't let you do it.

Michael: *(Passionately, almost berserk)* It's going to be done.

All: No. Never.

Michael: *(Shouts insanely)* Out of my path or somebody will get hurt.

(He swings the sledge. They break before him. With a cry, part anguish, part relief, he assails the wall. Heaving and groaning he smashes blow after blow on it. It cracks and crumbles before his onslaught. Finally when he has exhausted himself Paddy and Tom lead him to a chair. Lelum takes the sledge and puts it to one side. Michael sits with his legs extended. They lift him to a better position on the chair)

Mary: Will we get you a drink Michael? One of the boys will go.

Michael: No. Not now. *(He rises in spite of them and respectfully they allow his access to the exit)*

Mary: Are you all right Michael?

Michael: What would be wrong with me? I'm tired, that's all. I'll see you lads in the morning before you go. *(Looks at wall)* Everything will be all right in the morning. The good God always sees to that. God always comes up trumps in the morning.

(Final Curtain)

THE MAN FROM CLARE

The Man from Clare was first produced by the Southern Theatre Group on 1 July 1962 at the Father Mathew Hall, Cork, with the following cast:

Packey	Michael Twomey
Petey	Ber Power
Daigan	Dan Donovan
Cooney	Charles Ginnane
Frank	Pat Duggan
Jim Flynn	Flor Dullea
Padraic O'Dea	Michael McAuliffe
Bríd	Abbey Scott
Nellie Brick	Máirín Murphy
Morisheen Brick	James N. Healy
Elsie McDonagh	Irene Comerford
Other footballers	Seán Healy
	Noel Quinn

PRODUCER	Dan Donovan
DESIGNER	Frank Sanquest

This revised two act version of *The Man from Clare* was presented by Groundwork in association with Gaeity Entertainments at the Gaeity Theatre on 30 July 1992.

Pakey	Mark O'Regan
Petey	Liam Heffernan
Daigan	Mick Lally
Cooney	Risteard Cooper
Frank	Frank O'Sullivan
Jim Flynn	Conor McDermottroe
Padraic O'Dea	Brendan Gleeson
Bríd	Fionnuala Murphy
Nellie Brick	Ruth McCabe
Morisheen Brick	Johnny Murphy
Elsie McDonagh	Marina Ní Dhubhain
A Girl	Sonja Broderick
Other Footballers	Kieran Hurley
	Tim Murphy
	Andrew Bennett
	David Collins
	Cormac Costello,
	Daragh Byrne

DIRECTOR	Pat Laffan
DESIGNER	Brien Vahey
LIGHTING	Rupert Murray
PRODUCERS	Ben Barnes
	Arthur Lappin
EXECUTIVE PRODUCER	Ronan Smith

ACT ONE

Scene I

Action takes place in darkness, near the harbour of Cuas on the Clare side of the Shannon River on a May morning, with the dawn no more than minutes away. There is the light of a good moon where men might advance to be seen. A group of men are gathered in the half light, with bundles of football togs. One has a football, and another an accordion. They are the Cuas team from Clare, waiting for the motorboat which will take them across the river to play the annual match against the Bealabawn team from North Kerry. Two raw and awkward young men, Pakey and Petey, are in the centre of the stage. They are argumentative.

Pakey: Three years ago, when I was second sub, I was late through no fault of my own and the boat went without me. I was only a minute late and they were only just barely out from the pier at Bealabawn. I roared at them and I yelled at them and I screeched at them but they never put back for me.

Petey: You were tellin' me that before!

Pakey: I flung big rockers o' stones after 'em, an' they didn't even look behind.

Petey: There should be a rule about it!

Pakey: That's right! A rule is the thing. I'll propose it, if you'll second it.

Petey: Propose it so!

(Pakey rises and stands on minor elevation)

Pakey: Lads ... lads ... *(The hum of conversation dies.)* I propose a rule.

Petey: And I second it.

Pakey: Passed.

Daigan: What's the rule?

Pakey: The rule is that I was left behind three years ago and I was stranded in Kerry for a day and a night all on account of I goin' off with a carload o' girls to a dance in Abbeyfeale, and I propose that no one be left behind ever again an' that no man board the boat until every man is accounted for an' that way we'll all arrive home here together an' there'll be no need for awkward explanations to our women. That's the rule!

Petey: An' I second it!

Daigan: A vote! All in favour say 'Aye!'

(A number of 'Aye's are heard.)

Daigan: And now – who's against?

(There are no responses)

I see! Well, I'm against an' I'm dead against! I want to hear no more about that. When the boat is ready, we're ready an' any man that's late, we'll go without him, an' on top o' that I'll see that he's suspended for twelve months from the Club. What business have I tryin' to train you to be footballers if you're goin' to be out all night like a squad o' tomcats? The boat will be comin' back here four hours after the match. That's ten o'clock. You'll have four hours for drinkin', or courtin', or fightin', accordin' to your lights. Ten o'clock, I say ... sharp!

Pakey: Well, I object ... are you goin' to second me Petey?

Petey: Yerra, second yourself! I'm sick o' bein' second.

Voice: What's for the winners today?

Daigan: There's a set o' silver medals an' a cup for the Captain, and remember, when you're out on the field, the Captain has the last word. Whatever he says is law. All agree?

(Shouts of 'Aye!' 'Proper order!' etc.)

Now there's one more very important question to be decided

	before the boat comes, an' that's the question of Captain. I want no say in that, so 'tis up to yourselves.
Voice:	Padraic O'Dea, o' course …! Who else?
Voices:	'Yes, Padraic O'Dea!' 'A tried man!' etc.
Pakey:	I'm for Padraic O'Dea!
Petey:	And I'm for him, too.
Voices:	'O'Dea!' 'Padraic O'Dea!'
Voice:	With all due respects and no reflections intended, I think it's about time someone else got a turn. The captaincy should go round.
Voice:	But there's no one as good as Padraic an' we want a good captain.
Voice:	What about Jim Flynn?
Daigan:	Fair enough! For Padraic O'Dea, the Ayes?
Voices:	Aye!
Daigan:	For Jim Flynn?
	(There is no response)
Jim:	I didn't want to be captain anyway!
Pakey:	I'd never vote for anyone only Padraic O'Dea.
Petey:	Me the same!
Daigan:	Anythin' else on anybody's mind? No good talkin' about these things when we're in the middle o' the Shannon.
Voice:	If a fellow wanted to bring home a couple o' hundredweight o' good spuds, would there be room in the boat?
Daigan:	Out o' the question! I won't have it! The next thing you

know some fellow would want to bring home a cock o' hay, or an in-calf heifer.

Voice: Or a woman!

Voices: Aye!

Voice: Lively women in North Kerry!

Voice: Who's the referee today?

Daigan: He's a man called Driscoll, from Cork.

Voice: Couldn't they get anythin' but a Corkman?

Voice: Are we to get anythin' out o' the gate?

Daigan: They're payin' for the boat an' there's a free feed after the match, an' porter for anyone that wants it. They can't do any more, an' knowin' some o' the porter guzzlers in this team, they'll want a very good gate to pay for it.

Voice: Is the team picked?

Daigan: 'Twas picked last night ... Get up now an' gather round and I'll give you your positions.

(They gather round Daigan. A man comes from the crowd upstage, into the light, and begins to examine his compact arrangement of football boots, togs and stockings. He kneels while he goes carefully through his gear and calls: 'Padraic! ... Padraic!' to the background of conversation.
    A man advances from the crowd and stands over him. He too carries football gear)

Padraic: What ails you now?

Jim: I'm half in dread to tell you! I want to ask you something and I can't get it out of me.

Padraic: Why did you call me, then ...? Don't you know Daigan is advisin' the lads...? Come on! That's where you should be, too, listenin' to Daigan. Japers, man, if we're beat today it's the finish of us! *(Kindlier)* What are you doing out here alone, anyway?

Jim: I'm in dread ... I'll tell you no lie ... This is my first time playing the other side of the Shannon. I'm in dread of my sacred life of the Kerry lads. 'Tisn't afraid of what will happen to me at all, I am, but 'tis how I'm afraid I'll run an' leave the rest of ye down if there's crossness or boxing.

Padraic: You're not a coward are you?

Jim: I'm no coward and I'll hold my own with any fellow, but I'm afraid all the same.

(Padraic kneels down)

Padraic: Of course you are! Every man is a coward until he's cornered. Your courage will surface when the whistle sounds and the ref throws in the ball.

Jim: 'Tis aisy for you! You're the best man in Clare, Padraic, an' you're afraid of nothin' an' everybody knows you, an' no one will challenge you.

Padraic: Look Jim, boy! ... Football is a sport with blood in it, a sport of strength and hard hittin' and fair play: a sport with its own share of blackguards, but they're scarce and most of the lads are the same as ourselves. Look what football is ... 'tis goin' for the ball and doin' your best to get it. If you get a ball 'tis your ball and if a fellow tries to take it from you, take the proper proceedings against him. But never hit a man from behind, never blackguard a man that's weary and played out and, above all, never kick a man whether he's up or down, but if a fellow hits you a lick of an elbow or a belt of his bottom, belt him back or you've no business playin' football.

Jim: What about the ref?

Padraic: A ref has only two eyes so be your own ref when he can't attend to you.

Jim: What's it like over in Kerry?

Padraic: Over in Bealabawn, you mean? I don't know. I played there ten times, twelve times. I've half the games forgot. They always beat us on their own sod but we were never cowarded. That's the main thing. Bealabawn! 'Tis only a streel of a village with two pubs. Come on man, or Daigan will be like a devil!

Jim: Padraic!

Padraic: What?

Jim: If there's a row today will you back me? ... Well, will you?

Padraic: If 'tis a fair fight, you'll be on your own, but if a man is outnumbered or kicked when he's down, I'll be there ... fair enough?

Jim: Fair enough!

Padraic: Come on then!

Jim: Would you say there'll be a row today?

Padraic: How do I know? Look ... if a fellow puts a fight up to you, remember the first clout is the one that counts. A good early clatter into the gills and you have a fellow half-giddy before the fight starts at all.

(Daigan arrives upstage. He is a man with wild eyes and a head of wild grey hair)

Daigan: Did ye think I was speakin' to myself, or somethin', back there? Get up! ... In the honour o' God get up, an' wouldn't ye listen to my plan o' play?

(Others of the crowd gather nearer. To man in background)

Take the lantern, Pakey. We'll go to the boat now.

(A torch is lighted in background)

Once more, lads ... gather up an' sit down. *(They come around Daigan in a circle)* Any free kicks in their half of the field, you take them, and remember to get your heel back up to your arse when taking a free. If you don't get the heel back up to your arse you won't drive the ball. Did I ever tell you about Long Legs Callaghan from Killishen? Christ there was your kicker of a dead ball! One time they placed the football on a *triopall* of *fionnán* and he stood back from it, cocked his rear, smote it. The cover of that ball landed outside the presbytery in the town of Kilrush and the bladder landed outside the hall door of a whorehouse in Buenos Aires! You're a young team with the exception of Padraic here, an' he's wiser than any o' you. This team you're meetin', Bealabawn, they're crabbed an' crafty, an' they'll have players from all over North Kerry but they'll all be ancient footballers because there's nothin' good comin' up to them. Here's our plan. Hit 'em an' harry 'em an' keep hittin' 'em until they're tired. Wear 'em down first an' then play the ball well to the wings, so that they won't be able to run after it. Then lob the ball into the goals an' every man that's near, in on top of 'em an' no mercy. Are we right?

Chorus: Right!

Daigan: Who has the jerseys?

Voice: They're safe! I have 'em.

Daigan: We've nothin' to lose, an' it could be the first time in thirty odd years we beat Bealabawn on their own ground. 'Twould be an awful blow to them an' they always so cocky an' full o' gumption. Lads, we're not representin' Clare here today. We're only a club team but we are from Clare. I have seen good Clare teams and bad Clare teams but I have never seen a Clare team that was cowardly ... and I don't want to see one here today.

Voice: *(From the distance)* Hi, lads! Come on! The tide is right an' the engine is runnin'!

Daigan: *(Shouts)* Right! ... We'll be with you in a minute. One more thing, lads ... if it should happen that we're a few points ahead towards the end of the match, they'll do all in their power to start a fight. Don't hit back if you're winnin'!

Voice: What about the referee?

Daigan: A Corkman, is it? He'd enjoy nothin' better than to see
Kerry an' Clare fightin'!

*(They rise to their feet. They all stand fervently to attention.
A banner, held by two men, is visible with the slogan
'COME ON CUAS!' written on it. They form a sort of
company while a man with a melodeon starts into the tune
of 'The Men from Cuas'. The company marks time. After a
while, still marking time, they sing 'The Men from Cuas')*

All: Glory to the men of Cuas
The pride of the County Clare
In the rough or on the loose
The Cuas boys will be there.
Cuas boys here, Cuas boys there
Cuas boys, Cuas boys everywhere.
Cuas, Cuas, Cuas,
Cuas, Cuas, Cuas,
The men of Cuas are always there.

Now we go to play the game
To field the dropping ball
The men from Cuas will play it fair
Let each man give his all
Cuas boys here, Cuas boys there
Cuas boys, Cuas boys everywhere.
Cuas, Cuas, Cuas,
Cuas, Cuas, Cuas,
The men of Cuas are always there.

*(We hear their voices until they fade into silence. Padraic
and Daigan are about to follow)*

Daigan: Don't waste yourself in the first half, Padraic. Leave the
young lads do the work. Wait 'till the last quarter an' you'll
see gorgeous opportunities. Let yourself go then! Hammer
the goals with low balls an' we'll bring the Cup back to
Cuas tonight ...

Daigan: I have a feelin' we'll win today!

Padraic:	So have I!
Daigan:	What was wrong with young Jim Flynn? I saw you talkin' to him.
Padraic:	The usual ... I think he's afraid ... more nervy than anythin' else. He'll be all right when the whistle is blown an' the ball is thrown in.
Daigan:	I hope so. I hate fellows that have to work up their courage.
Voice:	Padraic! Daigan! Are you coming?
Daigan:	Come on, or we'll miss the boat.
	(They move away.)
Padraic:	Weren't you ever afraid yourself?
Daigan:	As big a coward as the next fellow, but that's not what I mean. Sure, there's nothin' to be afraid of in this world. I was only afraid of three things in my life.
Padraic:	What?
Daigan:	Rusty blades, casky porter an' parish priests' housekeepers ... Come on!
	(Curtain)

ACT ONE

Scene II

Action takes place in the kitchen of the house of Morisheen Brick in the village of Bealabawn in North Kerry. The time is near midnight of the day in question. Nellie Brick (Morisheen's daughter), a plain looking girl of 30, is sitting near the fire, darning socks. Near her is her young sister Bríd, a pretty girl, who is reading a woman's magazine.

Bríd: God! I'm jaded out!

Nellie: From doin' nothin'! Have you any notion o' goin' home? You're here a week now.

Bríd: I'll go when he comes for me.

Nellie: An' supposin' he don't come, what'll you do? Stay here with us for ever? If I know anythin', that's no way to treat a husband.

Bríd: If you know anything – that's just it! You don't know nothing! Sure, you were never with a man in your life!

Nellie: That's true!

Bríd: Sorry, Nellie! I didn't mean that.

Nellie: It's true, but it doesn't matter. Forget it! ... There's our father....

(Enter a bluff man with a crafty eye, of indeterminate age, in fisherman's garb. He carries a five-gallon container or bucket in his hand, staggers under the weight and is glad to leave it down)

Morisheen: Get up! Get up o' them chairs! We'll be havin' visitors in a few minutes.

Bríd: Visitors!

Morisheen: Footballers.

Bríd: Footballers!

Morisheen: The last footballer who stayed here was the mighty Elbows
                 Magennis from Miltown Malbay. He had an elbow like a
                 jackhammer. He blackened more eyes and more noses than
                 Jack Johnson. A nice fellow.

Bríd: Footballers this hour of the night! Are you mad?

Morisheen: Why aren't you in bed?

Nellie: Leave her alone. She's a married woman, father.

Morisheen: Sorry Nellie! *(To Bríd)* Go up there to the room an' get
                 ready the spare bed!

Bríd: You're not givin' me any orders!

Morisheen: God Almighty! 'Tis no wonder your husband is addled from
                 you. I swear on my oath I'll leather the daylights out o' you
                 if you don't do as you're told!

Bríd: I'm not goin' to be a skivvy for your drunken friends!

Morisheen: What's that? ... Go on, I'll...!

                 (Bríd does his bidding and exits)

Morisheen: She'd better modify or she'll be short a husband.

Nellie: The world will change her.

Morisheen: 'Tis the devil to see her married an' you scorned ... not
                 scorned, Nellie ... I didn't mean that!

Nellie: Why are ye all so careful not to hurt my feelin's? I wouldn't
                 care if I never married. You should know that by now Dad.

Morisheen: I know, Nellie, but if I had the way of it, 'tisn't a man I'd
                 pick at all for you but a prince.

Nellie: *(Pushes him away affectionately)* Oh, you ould clown, you!

Morisheen: Cripes! An' he'd surely make a knight outa me. Sir Morisheen Brick, Bart. 'Tisn't but I've royal blood in my veins as it is, better than any Sugarin' Bart-in-et, from your great-great-great-great-great-great-gra ndmother.

Nellie: Go on, with you!

Morisheen: Oh, that's a gospel fact! There she was, back at the time of the Armada, a handsome slip of a girl, with skin as smooth as an apple and black hair shiny like fresh tar, snug inside her bed when a tap comes to the window. 'Who's that?' says she. 'Open the window,' says the voice. ''Tis me, the youngest son o' the King o' Spain, an' my ship is sank, my little Irish Senorita!' 'Come in here out o' the cold,' says she, 'an' I'll warm you!'

Nellie: You'll have me believin' you soon! Now, what was this you were sayin' about visitors?

Morisheen: There's a brown flood in the Shannon: heavy rain today in the Midlands, an' freshwater wholesale after comin' in to it. There's a boatload o' Clare footballers high an' dry. I invited two of 'em down for the night. They'll be off with the first light o' day.

Nellie: Oh, the Cuas lads! What about the rest of 'em?

Morisheen: Gone off with women, or quartered in other houses ... They can be scourin' haysheds lookin' for 'em in the mornin'. You know the way them young hoboes scorn the bed and squeeze the last drop out of every hour of the night.

Nellie: An' are these two ould lads you're bringing here, or what?

Morisheen: Japers, no! One of 'em is Daigan the trainer, but the other fella is Padraic O'Dea, as fine a footballer as ever fielded a ball. You should see this man! Every bone well set in him an' a pair o' shoulders that would crack a stone wall for you. He's a quietly-spoken fella, too ... Like you, somewhat ... I'll bet anythin' he takes to you!

Nellie: Oh, for God's sake!

Morisheen: I'm serious! He's a fella that's advancin' well into years himself. You won't get a chance again ... By jingoes! If 'twas me I'd stop at nothin'. When I heard he was without a bed, I says to myself, that's the man for Nellie. Make the most o' your chances!

Nellie: What are you tryin' to say?

Morisheen: Nothin'...! Nothin' ... but it won't harm you to be polite to him.

Nellie: I'm always polite to people.

Morisheen: I know! ... I know! ... But 'tis like spoilin' a child ... wouldn't you put an extra bit o' jam on his bread if you wanted him to be fond o' you?

Nellie: Yes ... but how fond do you want me to be?

Morisheen: Ah, now you're making a mock o' me! ... Will that one below be able to tidy the bed all right?

Nellie: Ah, now Dad, give her half a chance!

Morisheen: Who's housekeeping for her husband, or does she expect him to hold a job and cook for himself as well?

Nellie: Ah, there's a neighbour o' theirs, a girl, that's keeping an eye to him.

Morisheen: Keepin' an eye to him, my tail! Good God, does she know anything about the world? Probably tryin' to get off with him ... when the cat is out!

Nellie: I suppose the pair that's coming will want something to eat. Is it a fry I'll put down for them or would they like somethin' cold? There's a fair share o' bacon left after the dinner.

Morisheen: Well, now, I asked them the same thing, an' they showed no interest at all in diet. Daigan the trainer it was that stuck a five-pound note into my hand and told me to order five gallons o' porter. Now, Daigan is a man who can be frightful pote-e-otic when he likes. 'When we're eatin', we're eatin',' says he, 'an' when we're drinkin', we're drinkin'!' ... I let it go at that.

Nellie: You would!

Morisheen: Isn't there enough arguin' in the world? Did you want me to start contradictin' them, an' they our guests for the night?

(There is a knock at the door)

Them are they now! There's a great name out o' these men for football. Show 'em respects, Nellie, because there's a lot thought of 'em at the other side o' the Shannon.

(He opens the door. Enter Daigan followed by Padraic who wears a light mackintosh over togs and jersey. He has a handkerchief tied about his head to ward off the rain, and he carries a bundle of clothes in his hands)

Morisheen: *(Shakes their hands)* Welcome! ... This is my daughter, Nellie ... she's single ... Nellie, this is Daigan out o' Clare, an' Padraic O'Dea, the footballer ... he's single, too.

(Nellie shakes hands with both)

Nellie: The two of ye are drenched wet. Shove up to the fire.

Daigan: Did you bring the porter?

Morisheen: 'Tis there, an' here's your change. But, lookit...! Ye'll have a tint o' this first. 'Twould bring you back from the dead!

(He locates bottle of poitín in wellington or wader)

Daigan: Good God! Are ye makin' that here now?

Morisheen: We only makes barely enough for the curin' of our own colds and cramps ... egg-stands, Nellie!

Daigan: You used to play one time ... 'tis the walk o' you I remember.

Morisheen:	I played down on you. I sold you six dummies, but I suppose you wouldn't remember that. Ye bate us the same day ... Ah! it's a long time ago. That's the only time Bealabawn was ever beaten by Cuas.
Daigan:	That's over thirty years ago! I was at a wake the night before that game and I was still staggering as I stumbled out onto that field.
Morisheen:	Right! An' ye could have won today, too! A bit o' luck an' ye had it.
Daigan:	Maybe!
Padraic:	Go on! Blame me if you want to. I know what they're all sayin'! One bad game, an' all the good games are forgotten.
Daigan:	There's no one blaming you. You should have been playin' full forward, that's all! You hadn't the pace for midfield.

(Nellie hands each a cup. Morisheen pours from the bottle)

Padraic:	*(Explanatory to Morisheen)* I have football to burn, and I got the chances today, but when I went about changin' gears there was no power in my knees. 'Tis a sad thing, man, to have the heart an' the temper an' to find the limbs failin' you at the crucial moment.
Morisheen:	I know what 'tis like, man! We all went through it. Didn't we, Daigan? ... Good luck!

(They toast each other and sup from their cups. The Claremen are visibly affected by the drink)

Daigan:	That wasn't made in a doctor's shop.
Morisheen:	You're right it wasn't!

(They each dip their cups into the porter gallon and swallow hastily)

Morisheen:	*(To Daigan)* Come on an' I'll get you out o' that wet trousers. Come on up to my quarters and I'll give you a dry

pair ...

(Taking their cups of porter with them Morisheen and Daigan depart by exit taken by Bríd. Bríd immediately enters)

Bríd: Who's that?

Nellie: This is Padraic O'Dea out o' Clare. This is my sister, Bríd. She's married.

Padraic: Soft weather!

(They briefly shake hands)

Bríd: Who's the lad gone up into the room with my father?

Padraic: That's Daigan. He trains us.

Bríd: He didn't even salute me! Such ignorance! Are they all like that in Clare?

Padraic: No! There's ones like you there, too!

Bríd: Very smart, aren't you? He's a right lookin' thick, then, your trainer!

Padraic: That's a brainy man, Missie.

Bríd: *(Heading in direction of her own quarters)* I don't care if he had the brains o' Paul Singer, he has the head of an eejit! *(Exits)*

Padraic: Fairly quick with the tongue, that one!

Nellie: I know where she got that. She's married to a man from Listowel, an' you know the kind o' tongues they have there. Listen – give me that bundle of clothes and I'll set 'em out to dry in front o' the fire.

(He hands her the bundle, which she unravels quickly)

Padraic: Are we trouble to you? We could have just as easy gone to a hay shed.

Nellie: *(Laying clothes over chairs)* No trouble ... there's a spare bed, an' sure, Daigan is a bit o' company for my father. They'll be goin' back now over the games that were played forty years ago.

Padraic: Do you follow the football yourself?

Nellie: I saw you playin' a few times. I often saw you better than you were today.

Padraic: Ah! So you spotted it, too. I'm goin' off a bit now. I shouldn't have been playin' out the field, anyway.

Nellie: That's what they all said.

Padraic: Who?

Nellie: Oh, the crowd lookin' on. They said if you were playin' inside in the forwards, you'd have scored a few goals.

Padraic: 'Tis aisy talk when the match is over.

Nellie: D'you want a mug o' porter?

Padraic: Aye, thanks!

(Nellie fills cup and hands it to him)

Nellie: 'Tis a wonder you didn't go to the dance like the rest of 'em or take up with some girl. I seen plenty of 'em there today.

Padraic: Ah 'sh, I never bothered my head about dancin', an' to tell you the truth I never courted a girl. Would you believe that – me thirty-five years and I don't know the taste of a girl's lips?

Nellie: What? Have ye no girls back in Clare, then?

Padraic: Plenty!

Nellie: And how come you don't care?

Padraic: It isn't that I don't care. I never remember a woman in our house. My mother died when I was a baby, my father died a year later, broken heart. I had no sisters, no aunts. Football was my brother and sister, my father and mother. I loved football. I lived for it ... I'd die for football ... once. Fielding a ball from a cluster of hands, talons, you might say, possessing it then, owning it, playing with it, nursing it until an opening came.

Nellie: And the man in the room beyond, Daigan?

Padraic: My uncle. He reared me, taught me all I know.

Nellie: But not about girls!

Padraic: No, no girls. Football only, no time for girls.

Nellie: Don't you have a woman to clean up, to tidy?

Padraic: He's housekeeper too, my uncle. He does all, we get on fine.

Nellie: Take the coat off you an' heat your body to the fire.

(He takes off his coat and hands it to her. He wears togs and jersey)

Is that some class of a new hat they have in Clare?

(Shamefacedly, he takes handkerchief from his head)

Nellie: Sit down ... I'll have the kettle boilin' in no time ...

Padraic: Tea is one thing I have no time for when I'm drinkin' an' Daigan is the same. One drink at a time, I say.

Nellie: Do you drink all the time then?

Padraic: Seldom enough! I drinks on Sundays and Holy days, fair days and patterns. I drinks then from morn 'till night and afterwards do be curin' myself for the rest o' the week. But no drink otherwise. 'Tis only to get out o' myself now an' again.

Nellie: What do you do for a living?

Padraic: Fisherman.

Nellie: What kind of a season are ye having?

Padraic: Not bad, not good!

Nellie: 'Tis bad enough to the west, by all accounts.

Padraic: Ah, there's a lot o' luck in fishin'!

Nellie: There's a scar in your hand. Did you come by that today?

Padraic: 'Tis nothin'!

Nellie: 'Tis nothin' now, but it could be a quare handful tomorrow. *(Takes his hand and examines it)* You're right. 'Tis nothin' but a scratch. You have strong hands!

Padraic: Your arms are white.

Nellie: What are you lookin' at?

Padraic: Goose pimples.

Nellie: What about them?

Padraic: Nothin'! Only if there's one thing I like about women 'tis goose pimples. 'Tis the little way they set off the skin.

Nellie: Some people think 'em common.

Padraic: There's nothin' like goose pimples. I never touched a goose pimple. *(Gently, barely touches her arm)* 'Tis the cold that drives 'em out, isn't it?

Nellie: That's what they say.

Padraic: That's what I thought.

Nellie: An' I thought you told me you usen't to bother with women!

Padraic: *(Leaving her hand go)* I know! I know! But I amn't blind either.

Nellie: What used you be doin' when you should be chasin' women?

Padraic: I don't know! Give us another cup o' porter an' I'll give you the full history o' my life.

(Nellie takes his cup and fills it. Enter Morisheen with two cups. As he enters he is shouting back to Daigan who does not appear)

Morisheen: *(Ignoring the couple)* An' there was another fella with a baldy head from Lisdoonvarna. He attacked the sergeant of the guards in Carrigaholt one night an' broke two plate-glass windows before they rounded him up.

Daigan: *(Unseen)* Casey.

Morisheen: Who?

Daigan: Thady Casey! A great man to field a greasy ball.

Morisheen: Hard thing to do!

(Morisheen fills both cups from the gallon)

(To Nellie and Padraic) Harder catch a comet than a greasy ball. *(Exiting carefully with full cups, stops and turns)* Easier catch a mackerel than a greasy ball, easier catch a mermaid ...

Nellie: *(To Padraic)* You were goin' to tell me about the time when you should be courtin'.

Padraic: Oh, courtin'! I've it half-forgot now, what I used to be doin'. There was a crowd of us half-wild around Cuas an' we used go gallivantin' like stray cats till cockcrow. We used take the gates offa their hinges an' hang 'em offa trees an' put common cars up on the roofs o' houses, or if the night was fine, peel off our clothes an' go tumblin' like cock-salmon in the salt-water ... an' if there was meadows convenient we'd go gallopin' over them in our pelts an' be rollin' like donkeys in the young grass, or maybe go coursin' for ten miles along the coast o' Clare till the wind gave out on us an' we were fit for nothin' but the bed. I suppose you'll say we were half-cracked?

Nellie: Gor! Ye were full cracked!

Padraic: That's gone now. That's for younger men and boys.

Nellie: You're still a young man.

Padraic: Time to think of hanging up my boots. My pace is ... vanished ... pace don't come back.

Nellie: You don't have to play midfielder.

Padraic: Once a midfielder, always a midfielder. I'd never be satisfied on the wing or in a corner. I need space. I need freedom.

Nellie: What will you do?

Padraic: I suppose you have a lot of fellows after you here in Bealabawn ...?

(Enter Morisheen followed by Daigan)

Morisheen: Gimme a *Ciotóg* for the penalty. A good *Ciotóg* would drive a ball through a stone wall.

Daigan: 'Tis time for bed, I'm thinkin'.

Nellie: It's ready for you down there.

Morisheen: Yerra, what's your hurry man? Sure we'll have a talk first. There's a pile o' people in Clare I want to be enquirin' about. What about that fella with the buck teeth that used to stand in goals for Kilkee?

Daigan: *(Abruptly)* Are you for the bed, Padraic or not?

Padraic: Go to bed, let you ... I'll stay here 'till the porter is finished.

Daigan: You'll get stiff sittin' there like that ... you'll be cramped.

Padraic: Ah, you know, don't you, that I can't sleep in a bed with anyone. I'd only be kickin' like a jennet an' turnin' an' twistin' all night.

Daigan: Take the bed so, let you, an I'll sleep there in the settle.

Padraic: No! I'm staying here 'till the porter is drank.

Daigan: Have sense man, an' take your sleep! Don't you want to be picked for Munster?

Padraic: I'll be sleepin' for the rest o' the week. You take your sleep.

Daigan: *(Imperatively, so that Nellie and Morisheen start)* Get up to that bed and stop that nonsense!

Padraic: *(Coldly)* Aisy, Daigan, aisy! I'm thinkin', an' I'm in a mood for deep thinkin'. There's a lot in my mind.

Daigan: *(To Nellie)* Go to bed, let you! You'll only be keepin' him awake if you stay talkin' to him.

Morisheen: *(To Nellie)* Take your time!

Daigan: Can't ye let him alone, the two of ye? Do ye want to wear the man out?

Morisheen: We're doin' nothin' to him! 'Tis you that's doin' all the talkin'. By Jacos! You'd swear he was a child in swaddlin' clothes, the way you're talkin' to him.

Daigan: I'll talk to him whatever way I want!

Padraic: Go to bed, Daigan!

Daigan: I will, but let them go first.

Morisheen: *(After a pause)* All right! But you're takin' great liberties in my house. It's a good job you were a footballer ... Good night, Padraic!

Padraic:	Good night! ... Thanks for the shelter.
	(Exit Nellie; and Morisheen after a hard look at Daigan)
Daigan:	What was that one sayin' to you?
Padraic:	Nothin' at all. We were just passin' the time.
Daigan:	What did you say to her?
Padraic:	Look, man, you'll have to stop this! I can't be accountin' for every word I say.
Daigan:	All right! All right! But don't take any notice o' these people. Nothin' would suit your man better than to see you latchin' on to the daughter. She'll be firin' herself at you. Women are no good, man!
Padraic:	Women are a sport I never took up, Daigan. But I'm gettin' a great notion for it, lately. I could hold my own at any game if I was shown how to play it, and if there was goals to be scored at it, I'd raise as many flags as any fellow, but there's no instructors for the game of women.
Daigan:	What's gettin' into you at all?
Padraic:	*(Angrily)* In the name o' God, leave me alone! Here I am, over thirty-five years of age and I hardly spoke ten words to a girl in my life.
Daigan:	Aren't we happy enough, man? We were never short of anything.
Padraic:	You might be happy, but I amn't! There I was, as contented as could be, talkin' to that girl and you come on and break it up!
Daigan:	That one!
Padraic:	Yes, that one! What's wrong with her? I know she's not a ravin' beauty, but she's nice and she's a fair girl to talk to an' I do be lonely sometimes, Daigan, for the company of a girl. I'd tell this to no one but you.

Daigan: *(Touched)* I'm sorry Padraic. I was only thinkin' of you ... I'm sorry ... wait 'till after you're selected for Munster, you can have the pick of 'em.

Padraic: I'll never be picked for Munster, not now. Didn't you see me today?

Daigan: One game only ... 'tis early in the season ... you'll be picked all right. This is your year. I know it, man. I feel it. I'll tell you the truth, though, I don't see what you want botherin' with women for. We have a contented house an' 'tis better to leave well alone. Is there some girl back in Cuas?

Padraic: There is not! There's a girl in my mind, though, a quiet, gentle girl that often kept me awake at night.

Daigan: Who is she?

Padraic: *(Annoyed)* Ah, she's no one! *(Tips his forehead.)* She's in here, man. That's what makes it tormentin'. I can't feel her or touch her. She's like a summer wind on the Shannon, fresh and clean and beautiful. I'd love to be stroking her hair in the moonlight maybe, down by the tide or to sit down with her somewhere quiet and study her face. What the hell do you know, Daigan? You never dreamed!

Daigan: Didn't I?

Padraic: Go on away to bed. I'm happy here.

Daigan: Be sensible, man, and take your night's sleep.

Padraic: *(Angrily)* I told you once, I told you twice, now I'm tellin' you for the third time ... I'm stayin' here. Go on away to bed now. I've a lot o' weight on my mind.

Daigan: If you change your mind, you can have the bed.

Padraic: All right! Only let me be!

Daigan: Change into your clothes.

Padraic:	All right! All right!
Daigan:	Good night!
Padraic:	Good night!

(Exit Daigan. Padraic gets himself another cupful of stout and begins to unlace his football boots. As he does so he begins to sing the song 'The Hills of County Clare'. Enter Bríd)

Bríd:	I don't suppose you heard anyone prowlin' around outside?
Padraic:	No … not a sound…. Were you expectin' someone?
Bríd:	Don't be funny!
Padraic:	I wasn't tryin' to be.
Bríd:	Well, I'm just tellin' you in case you do.
Padraic:	You think he'll come, don't you?
Bríd:	*(Guiltily)* Who?
Padraic:	Your husband.
Bríd:	What business is it of yours, I'd like to know?
Padraic:	No business o' mine, except …
Bríd:	Except what?
Padraic:	Except you'll have to bend your head a bit with the breeze if you want to get on with people.
Bríd:	I don't care if I never got on with people.
Padraic:	Signs by, you can't pull with your husband. That's your trouble.
Bríd:	Yes, it is my trouble, not yours. What do you know about trouble? You're not married.

Padraic:	I have troubles in my head, girl, and all the combs in the world wouldn't get 'em out of it.
Bríd:	Listen … will you do me a favour?
Padraic:	If I can!
Bríd:	You'll be here, won't you, till daybreak?
Padraic:	Yes.
Bríd:	If you hear him around the house, will you go out to him?
Padraic:	Why won't he come in?
Bríd:	He's too proud to knock.
Padraic:	An' what do you want me to do?
Bríd:	If you hear him is there any chance you'd go out an' capture him?
Padraic:	Is he wild, or what?
Bríd:	No … No, but hold on to him until I come out. Let out a roar and I'll hear you. Well, will you do it?
Padraic:	Right! … I can only be killed once!
Bríd:	Thanks!
Padraic:	But why don't you go home?
Bríd:	No hope!
Padraic:	He'll be glad to see you.
Bríd:	I wouldn't give him the satisfaction, and how do I know…? Maybe he won't want me.
Padraic:	He'll want you. Why wouldn't he?
Bríd:	Talk!

Padraic: What kind o' talk?

Bríd: Oh, neighbours that would be whisperin' about you if you passed the time o' day with another man.

Padraic: Hell isn't hot enough for anyone that comes between people that are fond of each other.

Bríd: That's the truest word you ever spoke. We could work out fine if we were left at it. We have our fights, but sure, everyone has them.

Padraic: What was this fight over?

Bríd: A silly thing.

Padraic: A sure sign that you're stone mad about each other.

Bríd: It was in the evenin' an' he was after comin' in from work. I poured out his tea an' some of it spilled in the saucer. He hates tea spilled in the saucer.

Padraic: So do I! ... Go on.

Bríd: 'Watch out the way you're pourin' that tea!' says he. 'You're awful particular!' says I. Then one word borrowed another an' I packed my traps an' came here.

Padraic: How long ago is that?

Bríd: A week.

Padraic: Time to be makin' it up.

Bríd: I'm lonely for him.

Padraic: Go to him! As soon as you rise tomorrow, get up on a bicycle an' go straight home. Walk in the door to him an' throw the two hands around him an' I bet 'twill be a long time before you get your wind back after the squeezin' he'll give you.

Bríd: Would you say that?

Padraic: I'll swear it to you on a stack o' bibles!

Bríd: You're sure!

Padraic: Certain!

Bríd: I'll chance it in the morning. I'll chance it. 'Twon't be my fault. I'm a terror with the tongue, amn't I? I can't help it. It breaks out in me like dancin' or singin' in someone else.

Padraic: Or football!

Bríd: I'll slip up to bed. Change into your clothes … and listen to me … I'm sorry your team were beaten today.

Padraic: We'll rise again.

Bríd: You look lonely there!

Padraic: I'm nearly always lonely.

Bríd: A man needs a woman in his life three times, they say.

Padraic: Three times?

Bríd: When he's a baby to rear him, when he's at the peak of his power to give him love, and when he's old to nurse him.

Padraic: No! No, you're wrong. I'm beginning to think a man needs a woman all the time.

(Curtain)

ACT ONE

Scene III

Action takes place as before. One hour later, Padraic is sitting by the fire with a cup of porter in his hand. He sings slowly to the air of the Cuas song.
Enter Morisheen, barefooted. He is coatless. He wears shirt and trousers.

Padraic: *(Sings)* Where shall I find the one I love?
A lady quaint and fair
As gentle as the cooing dove
With flowing soft brown hair.
I love her
I love her
Her loveliness I long to trace
I love her
I love her
Although I've never seen her face.

When shall I see my treasure trove
This lady quaint and fair?
When shall I walk beside my love
All through the land of Clare?
I love her
I love her
Would that she could hear my lay
I love her
I love her
I long to hold her night and day.

Morisheen: I knew a fellow from Carrigaholt that used to sing like that. He was a tall musty-lookin' fellow with a gullet like a crocodile. He'd swallow anything provided there was alcohol in it. Do you know many songs?

Padraic: Awisha, an odd one here and there. Sit up to the fire.

Morisheen: *(Filling a cup of porter)* Did you ever hear this one: 'There's nothin' like mate, said Paddy from Clare'? And another line; 'We'll be eatin' reheaters' *(pronounced ray-haters)* says Paddy from Clare'? Did you ever ate ray-heaters? Leftover boiled spuds you'd place among hot coals till the skin turned black. Then make a hole with your finger and drive in a blureen of butter. Food for angels, boy!

Padraic: I often ate them at night with a feed o' herrin's. Good fodder for a hungry belly.

Morisheen: Nothin' better! *(Sits down)* What kind of a fella would you take me for? Tell the truth now and take your time. *(Morisheen poses as though for a photograph)*

Padraic: A bit of a rogue, I'd say!

Morisheen: Great! Great! You're not far wrong. That's awful good that is – a bit of a rogue!

Padraic: A likeable rogue, though, with a tooth for a drop o' the hot stuff an' maybe now you're a man that would be no bad hand with the women. In fact, I'd say women would be pure putty in your hands.

Morisheen: *(Delighted)* The Gospel truth! … Go on …!

Padraic: I'd want to know you better, but I'd say one thing for sure …

Morisheen: What's that?

Padraic: You've more in your head than shows in your face.

Morisheen: I like that.

Padraic: You're a brainy man.

Morisheen: Yes, yes, but a brain without looks is like a pod without peas. Dear God, a brain without looks is like a barrel without porter. Would you say now that I'm a comely man, a presentable man? *(Preens himself)* Steady yourself now, take proper stock. Don't spare me now, let me have the naked truth.

Padraic: Well, you're healthy an' you're fresh an' you've a gamey eye. All things allowed, I'd say you're not a bad-lookin' young fella.

Morisheen: What age would you say I am?

Padraic: I haven't a clue, but 'tis certain you'll never play for the Kerry minors.

Morisheen: Well, I'll tell you! I left sixty some time ago an' now I'm a next-door neighbour o' seventy. But here's my trouble ... I have a powerful notion o' gettin' married again. Keep that under your hat. I've a strong notion, too, that I'd like to have a son ... I never had a son ... two daughters ... Nellie's an angel, but 'tis a son I'd like to have. I've great stories inside in me an' the most marvellous conglomeration o' painted lies you ever heard in your life but what's the good when I've no young fella to be tellin' 'em to? I'd apprentice him to every denomination of roguery an' humour so that he'd take the knocks o' the world in his stride an' break his behind laughin' at the invoices of misfortune.

Padraic: Yes ... but have you the mother o' the child picked out?

Morisheen: A noble an' a forthright question! Do you know Listowel well?

Padraic: I played a few matches there.

Morisheen: Do you know Cockatoo Lane at all there? It's only possessed of seven cottages, a duckhouse and two henhouses.

Padraic: I think I have it now. Is it the first lane on the left as you go into town?

Morisheen: The very place. Well, there's a one-storey house there with two cannisters o' purple geraniums in the window an' a coop for pigeons up on a pole in the back yard.

Padraic: I think I noticed it once or twice.

Morisheen: Well, she lives there with her brother. He's a postman, a famished ould perisher. 'Twould break his heart to give you a registered letter. She's a bit with the forty, but we have an understandin'.

Padraic: Have you spoken to her?

Morisheen: Not exactly, but I often gave her a wink an' she gave a wink back. If I got ten minutes alone with her an' told her the advantages o' bein' married to me, I'd be a certainty.

Padraic: What about her brother?

Morisheen: Won't he have his letters an' his parcels? What more does he want? An' look at all the Christmas cards he'll be deliverin' an' Goddamit, what's to stop him from pickin' up a wife himself on his rounds. Hasn't he recourse to women every day of his life and hasn't he a uniform. A lot of women collapse at the sight of a uniform with never a thought for the commodities underneath?

Padraic: Are you sure she'll marry you?

Morisheen: As sure as I'm talkin' to you! If she says no at first I'll pester her with parcels o' plaice an' whitin' an' another great plan is to saunter up an' down the lane outside her house until such time as she'll tell you come in or call the Guards. Man, dear, perseverance is a deadly weapon as far as women are concerned. I knew a widow one time from Cork an' she swore she'd never look at another man in her life the day her husband was buried. A month after, she was married to a fellow that used sharpen knives. He called to her door every day for thirty days an' sharpened all her cutlery an' never charged her a brown penny.

Padraic: Perseverance pays! You're sound in wind and limb?

Morisheen: Oh yes. Sound as a bell. A good man too around a house and a great man entirely in a bedroom. More porter?

Padraic: You took the words out o' my mouth.

Morisheen: *(As he fills cups)* D'you know what I heard an' ould schoolmaster o' mine say one time?

Padraic: Tell us!

Morisheen: He said porter in any shape or form is truly wonderful, and 'Maurice,' he said to me, 'the man that turns his back on porter for whiskey, turns his dial to the devil'.

Padraic: Did he now? I'd swear on my oath, your schoolmaster never said anythin' of the kind!

Morisheen: What does it matter what he said as long as someone said it?

Padraic: *(Accepting the cup of porter)* You're goin' gallant with the conversation but what made you get out o' the bed to come down to talk to me? I agree that there must be a certain amount o' roguery in the world. Now if 'tis roguery for a purpose, I'm all for it, but if 'tis needless roguery, you wouldn't blame a man for gettin' tired of it.

Morisheen: *(Sitting down and assuming a confidential pose)* You probably know what brought me down? You twigged it when you saw me comin'!

Padraic: I have a fair idea but of course a man can never be sure. State your case, anyway.

                 (They size each other up)

Morisheen: 'Tis a delicate subject. I'm slow about it.

Padraic: 'Tis about your daughter, isn't it?

Morisheen: Yes, 'tis about her. How did you guess?

Padraic: 'Tis written all over you.

Morisheen: No more quibblin' so! Are you interested?

Padraic: No!

Morisheen: Are you positive?

Padraic: Well I hardly know her. I'm not condemnin' her, mind you.

Morisheen: The two of ye seemed to get on well enough.

Padraic: Seemed is right. We hadn't much time to like or dislike. I ... I just can't look over a woman like that and say yes or no.

Morisheen: You're not decided?

Padraic: Is she?

Morisheen: Well, to tell you the truth, I didn't say a word to her yet. I couldn't say it to her....

Padraic: And don't ... I'm not keen ... She's all right ... She's very nice and she's full o' courtesy, but she's not the kind of a girl I had in mind ... do you get my meaning? The way I had it in mind was to meet an honest, fair good-lookin' girl after a match some evenin' an' instead o' goin' drinkin' porter with Daigan, I'd inveigle her into goin' to the cinema an' maybe if we took to one another I'd propose to her an' we'd settle into the makin' o' children afterwards.

Morisheen: Ah! So that's the way!

Padraic: That's the way. Well like yourself I'd like to do my own pickin' and choosin'. I have certain notions and I want them fulfilled.

Morisheen: Things don't ever happen that way! No one ever gets the woman they dream about. Too much dreamin' about women spoils a man for other women. A woman in the flesh is worth ten in the mind. Nellie is here under your hands, alive and well. Your dreamy woman is neither here nor there.

Padraic: True, true. But still a man would like to look around and find the nearest things to his dreams.

Morisheen: Do you know what's nice? Girls you'd see through the windows o' motorcars. They're here one minute an' gone the next. If you took them out o' the motorcars now they'd be just the same as ordinary girls as you'd see walkin' the streets.

Padraic: You miss nothin'!

Morisheen: I'll ask you once more ... are you interested in any way in Nellie?

Padraic: In no way whatsoever except to talk to her the same as any other human bein'.

(Enter Bríd with a small suitcase. She wears a coat and a headscarf)

Morisheen: What's this?

Bríd: What's what?

Morisheen: What's the idea o' the bag, an' the coat on at this hour o' the night?

Bríd: I'm goin' back to Willie.

Morisheen: How, might I ask?

Bríd: On Nellie's bicycle, or do you expect me to walk?

Morisheen: An' who's goin' to collect it?

Bríd: You can collect it the next day you come to Listowel starin' at the postman's sister. You could do tricks up on it in front of her house like a schoolboy.

Morisheen: You're a flamin' rip! No wonder your husband don't put up with you.

Bríd: *(Viciously)* An' whose fault is that, might I ask, but yours? 'Twas you rushed me into marriage the same way as you rushed Nellie into a convent so as you'd have the house here to yourself an' so's you could get married again.

Morisheen: If there weren't visitors in the house I'd turn you over my knee!

Bríd: Come near me an' I'll give you a welt o' this ... *(Swings suitcase)* ... you oul' gangster ... you oul' pirate ... no wonder you used be fillin' Willie with whiskey. Willie was fond enough o' me an' he'd have married me in due course if only you let well alone an' let things proceed naturally. But you couldn't wait. You rushed me into marriage when I was eighteen an' I havin' no qualification in the world for it, an' Willie worse again but we'll make out. I can thank this man from Clare because although he's the most ignorant man in the world with regard to women, he gave me a few honest answers. The next time you're inside with that oul' dexter from Cockatoo Lane, go down to the chemist's shop an' take a good dose o' Cascara. 'Twill do you more good in the long run.

(Exit Bríd)

Padraic: She's wise to go back to him.

Morisheen: I want no relation at all with a woman, only her company. You'd think I was a desperate ould dotard that did nothin' but chase women from the way she was talkin'.

Padraic: But don't you want a son?

Morisheen: If an accident happens in marriage ... who're you goin' to put the blame on?

Padraic: You're a bigger rogue than I thought you were.

Morisheen: You still like me though!

Padraic: Yes, I like you! But you see my position in the other matter don't you?

Morisheen: I'll go back to bed now an' reconcile myself to loneliness for the rest o' my life. *(Exiting)* You could bring me great happiness if you changed your mind.

Padraic: You're expectin' too much of me. Man I'm nearly a black stranger to you.

Morisheen I had a great song composed for the weddin' breakfast and I planned to spend the night of our honeymoon in Killarney. When I saw you today I said to myself there's a man that will save me from drownin' in loneliness.

Padraic: 'Tis tough!

Morisheen: There was a great prophecy related around here one time foretellin' wonderful events an' I thought when you came to the house tonight that you'd be part of it. I thought you were the man to bring the whole story true.

Padraic: I thought you were the biggest rogue in Bealabawn but now I'm thinkin' you're the biggest rogue in Ireland. What's the prophecy?

Morisheen: 'A man with a heart o' gold will swim the Shannon from Clare an' bring wonderful tidings to Kerry. A red-headed woman from Kilkee will give birth to a fiddler an' his music will convert Russia. An ass with an ear for music will be born in Banteer an' a man of seventy year will sire a noble son in the village of Bealabawn.'

(Curtain)

ACT TWO

Scene I

Action takes place as before. One hour later. Padraic sits, dressed, save for his small coat, which he holds across his knees. He would seem to be asleep. In the distance can he heard the melodeon playing 'God Save Ireland'. There are a few wild yells and whoops and the music grows louder and, suddenly there is a loud knocking at the door. Padraic stirs, rises, and goes to the door after repeated knocks.

Padraic: Who's that?

Voice: 'Tis me, Jim Flynn!

(Padraic opens the door and admits him. Enter Jim Flynn, who we will remember from the first scene when the boat set out from Cuas.)

Jim: We heard you were quartered here. Where's Daigan?

Padraic: He's asleep.

Jim: You missed a great night. You had a right to come with us. When the match was over, we took the banner – five or six of us – an' we followed a crowd o' girls as far as the town o' Listowel. We had a row there with a few o' the locals, an' we were arrested an' taken to the Barracks.

Padraic: What happened?

Jim: A couple o' size eleven boots in the rear end.

Padraic: They left ye go!

Jim: Well, the sergeant said: 'Which would ye prefer, a night in the cells or a few rooters in the behind?' *(Rubs his behind)* Them oul' guards know how to give a kick in the pants ... Boy, let me tell you!

Padraic: What time will the water be ready?

Jim: About four hours, he said. 'Tis droppin' fast and there's a moderate tide in the morning.

Padraic: Sit down an' rest yourself.

Jim: Rest be damned! There's a crowd o' the local girls outside an' they know an oul' barn where we can have a bit of a dance. We have the music. Come on, man: we'll only be young once.

Padraic: I can't dance. Anyway there's the most of a gallon o' porter here an' I couldn't go without finishin' that ...

Elsie: (Off) Jimmy! Jim Flynn!

Jim: I'll be with you in a minute.

Padraic: I wouldn't want to go anyway.

Jim: We had hard luck today. Beaten by a bare point. I thought we had them there for a while.

Padraic: 'Twasn't your fault. You had a great game. There was nothin' to hold you. If we had a few more like you we'd have won well.

Jim: I never played better. What happened to you today?

Padraic: The same thing that'll happen to you some day. After a half an hour your bones will start creakin' like rusty hinges, (Jim laughs) an' you'll think there isn't enough air in the whole world to fill your lungs when the wind gives out on you. You're grand now. You're at your best. You're a cock o' the walk. For a few years you'll think that you're the strongest man that ever wore a jersey an' then suddenly one day you'll be running for a ball an' a young fella will pass you out an' you know 'tis time to hang up your boots. 'Tis sad, man, to be beaten by a fella that wouldn't hould a candle to you one time.

Jim: If I didn't know you, I'd say you were jealous o' me.

Padraic: Not jealous Jim, but I envy you because your best years are before you and mine are away behind. They're tied around my legs, holdin' me back … The spirit is there all right. I'll never lose that and the jizz and the restlessness are inside of me but man, you can't fight the years and you can't match youth.

Jim: That's quare oul' talk! 'Tisn't like you!

Padraic: I'm changing, Jim. You mightn't understand it if I told you my heart was held back by my knees. Do you know what I'm going to tell you? I couldn't care less about football this night.

(Enter a young girl, Elsie)

Elsie: Are you coming, Jim Flynn? The night is lightening and soon the dawn will be here and 'twill be too late for dancin'.

Jim: In a minute.

Elsie: Come on! They're all gettin' impatient outside.

(She goes to him and links his arm possessively)

Padraic: They used be after me too like that once but I never bothered with 'em.

Elsie: Who's he, Jimmy? Was he playing today?

Jim: *(Incredulously)* You're not tellin' me you don't know? Sure that's Padraic O'Dea. Everyone knows Padraic O'Dea. He was playin' centrefield today.

Elsie: Was he?

Jim: But surely you saw him today.

Elsie: If he was any good I'd have noticed him. Now come on away to the dance. My feet are itching to rise dust.

(There is the sound outside of the melodeon playing the same march, and the melodeon player enters, playing. He is followed by two men, one with football boots tied about his

neck. They carry a banner between them which when unfolded reads: 'CUAS!' They are Pakey and Petey Mannon, Cooney is between them.)

Pakey: *(Shrilly)* Up Cuas!

Petey: *(Rebelliously)* To hell with Bealabawn!

(Both yell and whoop loudly)

Padraic: In the honour o' God, pipe down or you'll wake what's in the house!

Petey: *(Noticing gallon, sniffs it)* Jacos, Pakey, porter!

Pakey: Are you in earnest?

Petey: *(Gazing into gallon)* It has the black sudsy appearance o' porter. It has the strong stiff character o' porter an' it has the beautiful nourishin' smell o' porter *(flinging the ban-ner aside he puts gallon to his mouth and swallows)* an' it has the toppin' toothsome taste o' porter.

Pakey: Here, give me a cup out of it. I've a squadron of frogs' whelps in my windpipe from roarin' an' screechin'. *(He takes gallon and puts it to his head and swallows)* Thank God for all things wet ...

All: Amen! Good luck and success to the Council of Trent who put fast on the meat but not on the drink!

Pakey: Padraic, you oul' devil, what are ye doin' here out o' the way? We've women outside an' a barn got for dancin' an' there's four hours before the boat leaves.

Petey: An' there's a stepdancer's moon in the sky. Come on away man an' dance the kinks out o' your muscles.

Elsie: Yerra leave him there if he don't want to come. He has the appearance of a fellow that would cut the toes off a girl. Who is he anyway?

Pakey/Petey: *(In total disbelief)* Who is he? Sure the world knows him.

(Enter Morisheen in a long nightshirt)

Pakey: Is it a man or a woman?

Petey: 'Tis neither. 'Tis a hoor's ghost.

Morisheen: What's all the commotion?

Padraic: There, now! I told ye that ye'd wake the house up.

Morisheen: Did they wake you, Padraic?

Padraic: I was only dozin' anyway.

Morisheen: *(To Pakey, Petey and Jim)* I saw ye playin' today. I wouldn't trust either one of ye with a penny balloon.

Elsie: *(Clinging to Jim)* An' here's the best footballer in Clare.

(There is a shocked silence while they all look at Padraic)

Well he is, an' he proved it today! Come on Jim boy, they're all mad jealous of you.

Morisheen: You're Elsie MacDonagh, aren't you?

Elsie: That's right I am!

Morisheen: You should be in bed this hour o' the mornin'! When your mother was your age she was never out after ten.

Elsie: We're goin' dancin'. Will you come? You have a lovely outfit for it!

Padraic: Don't be disrespectful now to an old man. Shame for you and you under his roof!

Morisheen: Don't mind her, Padraic, you're wasting breath.

Elsie: You'd better be quiet, Clareman, or I'll give you a piece o' my mind too!

Morisheen: A piece of nothing is worth nothing.

Elsie:	Very clever, aren't you, but as smart as you are the whole village knows your cuteness. *(To all)* He has two daughters. One of 'em is always fightin' with her man an' the other one has no man to fight with.
Morisheen:	Shut up, you hussy!
Elsie:	And what does he do? *(Indicates Padraic)* He brings along your man here to know would he pawn the daughter over on him. A nice lob she'd have in you, an' you'd be in a nice way with her an' she in a convent for years but she couldn't stick that either, so she came away out of it. *(To Morisheen)* There now fox, that'll teach you to give lip to me!
Morisheen:	You're a flamin' hussy!
Padraic:	That's a terrible way to talk to a man in his own house. You show scant respect. What's the country comin' to?
Morisheen:	You're right there Padraic. Good on you Boy!
Elsie:	Are you goin' to let him talk to me like that, Jimmy?
Jim:	You can't talk to her that way!
Padraic:	Why not?
Jim:	I say so.
	(Enter Daigan wearing his clothes but bare-footed)
Daigan:	What's this?
Elsie:	Great God! What sort of a collection have you here at all? Is it a shop you have for repairin' ould crocks?
Daigan:	Jim, get that rip out o' here!
Elsie:	I'm no rip!
Daigan:	Maybe not, but you're a forward young devil, whatever you are.

Jim: There's no one goin' to talk to her like that while I'm here.

Daigan: Do you know where you're talkin' young fellow?

Pakey: Come on away dancin', Jim!

Petey: That's right, Jim: we'll have a bit o' sport.

Melodeon Player: Come on, Jim, and don't spoil the night!

Daigan: If he wants to go in one piece, he'd better go now.

Melodeon Player: Come on Jim.

Jim: *(Pleading)* How can I go when I'm spoken to like that?

Pakey: Come on Jim.

Petey: You've a few drinks taken.

Padraic: Go on dancin', Jim, an' forget it! We'll all be friends back home in Cuas tomorrow an' you'll have that one forgotten.

Jim: Don't you tell me when to go. You weren't so hot today yourself. Only for me we'd be beaten twice the score. You left us down.

Voice: Take it aisy Jim.

Jim: You were supposed to be our star. You were advisin' me how to play this mornin' an' I listened to you an' I said to myself, 'Take note of that, Jim, let you because that's Padraic O'Dea talkin' an' he's a man that should be noted an' respected', but no – you flopped an' you flopped because you didn't try your heart out like you're always tellin' others to do.

Petey: That's not fair Jim.

Voice: Ah, will you take it aisy.

Padraic: What's gotten into you Jim? We used to be pals, you an' me. Is the matches we played an' the trainin' we did to be all forgotten in one bit of a night because a strange rip of a girl from North Kerry wants to see two men fightin' over her?

Elsie: Don't call me a rip!

Jim: Don't call her a rip ...! *(Louder)* ... I said don't call her names. She's talkative an' all that, but she's a decent girl, so don't call her names.

Padraic: What's said is said. You know me. I don't backtrack.

Jim: Don't you? Well, you backtracked today and there'll be a new captain after the next meetin'. You can ask any o' the lads if you don't believe me.

Padraic: An' you'll be the next captain, I suppose....

Jim: Go on ... ask them.

Padraic: Is that right, Pakey ...? Is it, Pakey? ... well is it...? You, Petey, is that what the lads are sayin'? *(To melodeon player)* Frank, is this the talk ... is there to be a new captain? *(They are all noncommittal and somewhat hangdog.)* 'Tis the same in all jobs I suppose, when a man has his best given, he's kicked out an' pensioned off to make way for new blood – only there's no pension for footballers!

Jim: 'Tis what the lads want!

Elsie: He's a better man than you!

Padraic: Is he? Are you Jim ...? Are you a better man than me, Jim? It's no good sayin' it to yourself because the only one that'll believe it is yourself. If you want other people to believe it, you'll have to say it in public. Here's a chance to make a name for yourself!

Daigan: *(Coming and standing between them)* Have sense, lads! This bloody farce has gone far enough. Go on away to the dance, Jim. I take back what I said about your girl. We're all a bit irritated after today. Things didn't go right for any of us.

Jim: *(Pushing him aside)* Well, things didn't go badly for me today. Some said I was as good a man as ever came out o' Clare.

Daigan: If there was a way o' knowin' in the mornin' what way things would be in the evenin', we'd lock our doors an' come out from our kitchens no more!

Jim: Let that be the end o' your sermon now, Daigan. Padraic, for the last time, are you goin' to apologise to this girl?

Padraic: *(Calmly)* I can't apologise now, Jim, don't you see? It isn't the girl any more, or it isn't you or me. It seems to have grown up to be a big thing while we were talkin'. It's awful sad in a way.

Jim: *(Angry)* What are you talkin' about ...? What's awful sad?

Padraic: I don't think you'd understand! ... I don't think there's anyone could understand.

Jim: Well, understand this, Padraic ... *(menace)* ... I'm puttin' it up to you ... I'm askin' you to say you're sorry to this girl, an' if you don't, I'm askin' you to step outside an' I'll fight you to a finish.

Padraic: I don't want to fight you. Man dear, what good would that do either of us?

Jim: Well, say you're sorry so, an' we'll have done with it.

Padraic: She's the one that should be doin' the apologisin'!

Jim: *(Tensely)* All right so ... come on outside!

Padraic: No ... what does it matter? I was a great footballer for years an' what does that mean now? If I fight you tonight, will it make me a better footballer and what will it mean tomorrow?

Jim: Are you funkin' me?

Padraic: I am!

Daigan:	*(Shocked)* Padraic ...! What are you sayin' man? Are you gone mad?
Padraic:	I'm funkin' it ... I'm not goin' to fight. He'd beat me anyway. A few years ago I'd have murdered him. Go away Jim an' find another young buck like yourself. You won't make much of a name for yourself out o' me. I was beaten today when my knees failed.
Jim:	You're yellow!
Padraic:	If that's the colour they give a man who doesn't want to fight, then I'm yellow.
Jim:	You're a coward!
Padraic:	Am I two things now?
Jim:	I offered you fair fight an' you funked me. You're yellow!
Pakey:	We saw one this evening in Listowel, an' she was blue!
Elsie:	Shut up, you clown you!
Pakey:	We did ...! We did! Ask Petey.
Petey:	We did an' comin' out o' the barracks.
Pakey:	'Twas the sergeant's wife, she was trimmin' blossoms in the little garden in front o' the barracks. 'Are you foreign or a Mohammedan or what?' says Petey to her. 'What are you sayin'?' she said. ''Tis that blue head o' hair,' says Petey; 'we never saw the likes o' that in Cuas.' *(Nudges Elsie)* An' d'you know what it was? 'Twas a blue rinse for four pence she bought in a shop ...
Voices:	*(Offstage)* Come on out, if ye're comin' dancin'...! Come on an' bring the melodeon ... Ah, come on can't ye. We have a fiddler here from Lisselton and a drummer from Doon.
Elsie:	Come on Jim ... You're the best man in Clare an' you proved it tonight.

Morisheen: Is it long since you looked in a mirror?

Elsie: Why? … Why? What's wrong?

Morisheen: Didn't anyone ever tell you that you have a jaw like a narrow black pudden, a pair of ears like the wings of a sidecar an' a nose like the yolk of a goose-egg an' as ignorant an' as thick a skull you wouldn't find if you went rootin' through the graveyards of Ireland lookin' for specimens.

Jim: *(To Elsie)* Come on! Come on! He's only needlin' you.

(Jim drags Elsie towards the door)

Morisheen: *(Shouting after them)* An' a poll on the crown o' your head like one o' them hairy baboons you'd see eatin' bananas in Duffy's Circus.

Jim: You funked it Padraic … You funked me. 'Twill be the talk of Cuas tomorrow … That I cowarded Padraic O'Dea.

(Exit Jim and Elsie followed by Frank)

Morisheen: Anybody that knows Padraic O'Dea knows he isn't a coward.

(Pakey and Petey begin to ready their banner for the exit)

Pakey: *(To Petey)* Is there any more left in the gallon?

Morisheen: *(Snatching the gallon)* If there is, 'twill go to the man that bought it.

(Gallon in hand, Morisheen critically surveys Petey and Pakey. He walks around them, surveying them from head to toe. He pauses then, slightly to the side of them, staring at them intently)

Pakey: Why are you starin' at us?

Petey: Yes … that's the lookin' he has at us! You'd think we were racehorses or somethin'!

Morisheen:	Well racehorses is one thing an' donkeys is another thing an' anyone can see that you aren't racehorses!
Petey:	What's all the lookin' for?
Morisheen:	*(Still surveying them critically)* 'Tis hard to tell ... *(mock puzzlement)* ... very hard to say which it is.
Pakey:	Which is what?
Petey:	What is which?
Morisheen:	It has me puzzled since the two of ye walked into the house.
Pakey & Petey:	*(Retreating towards the door)* What? ... What?
Morisheen:	Which of the two of ye is the bigger eejit?
Pakey:	*(Whoops first)* Up Cuas! Glory, Cuas!
Petey:	Down with Bealabawn! To hell with Bealabawn! ... Herrin'-chokers an' pratey-snappers....

(Then with a series of wild yells, they are gone, singing 'The Cuas Boys')

Morisheen:	They're not brokcn in at all yet ... shouldn't be let out for a few more years ... Don't take any notice o' that girl. She's a thunderin' hussy since she went workin' to Listowel. Would you like to take my bed for a while, Padraic?
Padraic:	No thanks!
Daigan:	I never thought I'd live to see the day Padraic O'Dea was cowarded. Your name will be mud in Clare, to be cowarded by young Jim Flynn and he no more than a boy! I didn't think there was a man in the globe could walk up to you an' call you yellow.
Padraic:	Not makin' you a short answer, he can call me whatever he likes.
Morisheen:	Young cocks always crow the loudest. Why bother with

him?

Daigan: Of course he'd beat you. He's a faster man and he's at his best an' you aren't but that doesn't give you any call to back down.

Padraic: That wasn't why I backed down. Look, Daigan, I'm after resolvin' somethin' to myself an' in a way I'm contented. I want to hear no more about it now or you'll find me losin' my temper.

Daigan: The man you should have lost your temper with is gone out the door. If you want to lose it there's still time to follow him and put it up to him and fight until you're not able to stand up any more and that way you'll keep your good name and I'll be able to keep my head high when I go back to Cuas.

Padraic: Go to blazes!

Daigan: What?

Padraic: That's what I said! Go to blazes an' stay there. You're only worried about yourself. It don't matter a hang one way or the other to me, man, what anyone thinks. I'll have tears o' my own to be sheddin' tomorra an' I can see no one puttin' their hand on my shoulder an' sayin' 'Cheer up Padraic, you were a prince among men one time'.

Daigan: There's still time to go after Jim Flynn an' make him eat his words. You can beat him if I let him have an odd one from behind. I'll sidle in with a quick one when he isn't looking.

Padraic: That's not my way o' fightin'. I'd never stoop to that.

Daigan: (*Contemptuous*) Go away then with your tail between your legs.

Padraic: Go to bed, Daigan, or by the Lord God that made me, I'll crack your jaw! Don't pester me like an oul' woman, or I'll go for you!

Daigan: I've given you up! I don't know what's happened to you.

Padraic: Listen to me, Daigan. My football days are over. My strength is left to me but my timing is gone and my pace is squandered. I was the finest athlete in Clare but now I'm finished I'm just an ordinary fisherman. That's my lot. I'll never be shouldered off the field again. I'm lucky to have my fishin'. I'll go out now an' I'll fight Flynn, not for you Daigan, or not for my own pride. I'll fight him because it was to be. I want room for my boat when I pull into the pier at Cuas an' room on the strand for my nets to dry an' room on the fishin'-banks for my haul – otherwise I'd be pushed out an' that'd be the end o' me. *(Rolls up his sleeves, spits on his hands and flexes his fists)* You taught me Daigan. Close up your fists until you make weapons out o' them. Remember! Squeeze your fingers into a ball o' bone an' put your shoulder behind every clout so that when you hit a man his head will ring an' he won't come lookin' for more. *(Pitifully, then almost on the verge of tears)* Because don't you see, I'm a man out o' the village o' Cuas an' there's this jizz, this terrible bloody jizz inside o' me. I can't lie low like others and I can't cry my troubles out loud like a woman. I'd as lief be dead as be the way I am now.

(Padraic goes slowly out the door. Daigan moves to follow but Morisheen gestures him to stay back and both men look after the retreating figure)

(Curtain)

ACT TWO

Scene II

Action takes place as before. Time – Daybreak. From barn down the road comes the sound of a sleepy waltz. Daigan enters.

Daigan: There's no sign o' Padraic, I suppose?

Nellie: No ...! When I came down into the kitchen he was gone. Strange, isn't it, that he should go off like that? He didn't take his gear with him.

Daigan: He'll be back.

Nellie: Maybe he went down to the dance.

Daigan: No ... no ... not Padraic.

Nellie: Will you take a few eggs with your breakfast?

Daigan: No, I'll just take a cup of tea 'till Padraic comes ... D'you hear that music? Do they think that music is the only thing in the world? Music won't fill a hatch with herrings or open drills for potatoes.

Nellie: Aye, I heard them, they're at it all night long.

Daigan: It's a disgrace! Music, dancing, courting and roars out of them. Smoke-filled halls like dungeons ... and women that couldn't boil an egg for you.

Nellie: They might as well enjoy themselves. Soon enough they'll have to face the world. Dancing is harmless.

Daigan: A couple o' more nights like last night an' my lads wouldn't beat a team of oul' women. The music is stopped. It couldn't last. They started off with hornpipes and jigs an' reels, then Sieges of Ennis, then quick-steps an' waltzes an' now they're finishing up with slow waltzes.

Nellie: Everythin' wears itself out.

Daigan:	There are some things that don't.
Nellie:	What for instance? All things last their proper length.
Daigan:	The sea! Ships get weary an' men get weary, footballers get weary. Even the rocks do be worn away but the sea never gets weary. You couldn't tire the sea. I wonder what's happened to Padraic. The sea never sleeps and you'll never see the sea without life. Where the hell can he be? *(Rises)*
Nellie:	You sound worried!
Daigan:	*(Nervously)* I'm not! ... I'm not! ... Why should you go an' say that? What's there to be worried about? ... I'm not worried ... I was never worried about Padraic. You've no right to say that.
Nellie:	Sorry!

(Enter Morisheen)

Morisheen:	Ah! There you are Daigan ... Did you sleep well?
Daigan:	I only slept in patches. That bloody music kept wakin' me up.
Morisheen:	You forgot to say your prayers – that's what happened!
Daigan:	Must you be always so damn smart?
Morisheen:	I can't help it if you didn't sleep. What did you want me to do? Go up to the bed and sing 'Clare's Dragoons' 'till you dropped off?
Daigan:	I'm always remindin' myself that no one should pay attention to a fool an' here I am, listenin' to you!
Morisheen:	Where's Padraic? ... Isn't he back yet?
Daigan:	I'll be goin' out now in a minute to see would I find him.
Morisheen:	Why don't you leave him alone for a change?

Daigan: Mind your own business.

Morisheen: Let him alone! He's a grown man. You're breathin' down
                     the back o' his neck for years. He can't go left or right
                     without your approval. He has a life of his own to live,
                     especially now.

Daigan: What are you talking about?

Morisheen: You want him to be all the things you never were. You
                     failed at football yourself and you tried to turn Padraic into
                     the greatest ball player of all time. You should know what
                     the years do to footballers, Daigan, what they've done to
                     Padraic. The years have outfielded him at last, outstripped
                     him, left him stranded.

Daigan: He was a genius, I tell you, a genius. No one had his craft.

Morisheen: Aye! But geniuses are quare people. They're to be pitied
                     when time takes it all away. They can't ever knock at the
                     door and come in to the happy crowd and be part of it. No,
                     they have to keep company with other things – things like
                     the wind, and the rain and the sea – the most sorrowful
                     things. Leave Padraic alone, man, in the honour of God an'
                     he'll come around. But he must work it out for himself.

Daigan: *(Furious)* You schemin' connivin' oul' hypocrite! You're
                     the one that had the biggest plan of all made for him. You
                     thought you had nothin' to do but bring him here to the
                     house, an' this one here, this ex-nun with the shiny face that
                     you'd imagine butter wouldn't melt in her mouth. There's
                     women in Clare would fall at his feet if he bothered to pass
                     the time o' day with 'em, an' you fancyin' you were fit for
                     him. Gor! 'tis the joke o' the year ... I could die with the
                     laughin'!

Nellie: *(Hurt)* What started all this? I never saw him before last
                     night. I don't care for him an' I don't want him.

Daigan: Don't you though! You'd stop at nothin' to get him. I saw it
                     written all over you. You were well primed by that oul'
                     villain over there. You knew you had an innocent boy with
                     no knowledge at all of women. You'd draw the line at

nothin' if you thought you could have him. A reject, that's what you are ... a bloody reject ... You couldn't stay with the nuns because you were gettin' restless, gettin' anxious for the world. You couldn't sleep nights so you left and you came home to Dad. But Dad didn't want you either. Dad had different plans entirely.

Morisheen: For God's sake, stop it, man!

Daigan: *(Now in a frenzy)* What sort o' fools did you take us for? Did you think we passed up marriageable women in all the towns of Ireland to come here an' be fooled by a woman like you that will be old and grey in ten years?

Morisheen: Well, if she'll be old and grey in ten years, you'll be growing daisies in less.

Nellie: Stop it! Please, stop it! This is all wrong. This is a mistake.

Daigan: It's the truth, you bitch. Nothin' would suit you better than to chain my fine boy.

Morisheen: Your boy? He's not your boy! You don't own him. You're ruining him ... your boy.

Daigan: I reared him an' trained him an' taught him all he knows. I spoon-fed him and washed him with those two hands since he was a child. I never let a woman near the house to wash or cook for us. I did it all myself.

Morisheen: An' for all you taught him does he know happiness? Does he know peace of mind? The poor fellow can't even think for himself. I know he'll never take Nellie but he wouldn't get a better woman if he searched 'till he dropped an' that's one thing I mean from my heart because I know Nellie and I know the kind of girl she is.

Daigan: An' so do I an' I'll tell her! You're not good-lookin'! You're not well-made an' you're backward. Your manner is dull an' your wits are slow an' deny it if you like. There might be a man for you somewhere but Padraic O'Dea isn't that man.

Nellie: *(Broken)* I'm not denyin' myself. You painted a true like-
ness o' me. There's no place for girls like me, is there? The
like of me were born to mind other people's children or to
sit in a corner out of the way. But what about the girls like
me, the bashful girls, the dull girls, the withdrawn girls?
Who's to write lovesongs for us? Is it because we don't
present a fair picture on the outside that there's nothin'
inside of us? What do you want me to do? Go away an'
drown myself? There's a place for people like me too. God
wouldn't have made ordinary girls and shy girls unless He
had plans for us. It's because we are the way we are that
nobody will ever know our great capacity for love.

Morisheen: You're too good for him, Nellie.

Daigan: *(Indicating Morisheen)* An' I suppose God has plans for him
too? *(To Morisheen)* You couldn't give her away for
nothin': if you gave a million pounds with her, you wouldn't
get a dacent man to take her.

(Nellie bends her head into her hands)

Morisheen: *(Infuriated, takes a knife from the dresser)* Here take that
an' stick it through her! Go on man: why are you lookin' at
it? Take it an' ram it into her an' finish off what you started
… Go on! … She won't feel it after the stabs you've given
her already. Look at her bleedin' man! *(Shouting)* Look into
her heart an' you'll see the blood floodin' out of it like an
ebb tide … look into her eyes an' see the hurt that's in them
… no, you couldn't see … not you – you're blinded by your
own bitterness.

Daigan: *(Recoils confused)* Padraic … I've got to find Padraic.

*(Morisheen turns his attention to Nellie who is still bent
over the table)*

Morisheen: *(Disgusted)* You don't want to take any notice o' what that
fellow said. The world is full o' bitter men like him. He's all
twisted up for the want of a woman. Listen to me! Listen to
me … We'll be happy here, the two of us. We'll have each
other for company. Nellie girl, don't take on like that.

(Nellie raises her head and dries her eyes)

Nellie: What's for me Dad? What's to become o' me? I have nowhere to go.

Morisheen: You'll be all right, Nellie. I'll care for you.

Nellie: You will, an' are you goin' to live for ever?

Morisheen: You'll have Bríd. She'll be glad of you.

Nellie: And be a nursemaid to her children. When the children are grown up, where am I then? Who'll want me, Dad? I'll be alone.

Morisheen: I'll be here for years yet.

Nellie: No, you won't. It wouldn't be fair to you. I know all about that woman in Cockatoo Lane. You'll be pinin' for her all the time. Don't worry! You think I don't understand? I'll go housekeepin', that's what I'll do ... I'll go housekeepin' for a priest. I have to look out for myself ... I've let it go too long.

Morisheen: You'll go nowhere. You'll stay here with me.

Nellie: No ... that's what I'll do. My mind is made up. I'll housekeep for a priest in some quiet parish where I won't be known.

Morisheen: That's nonsense! I won't have that an' that's final ... I've been a quare father, haven't I, Nellie? Well I won't be so. You'll be happy here. You don't know the humour that's in me if I want to try. I'll have you in stitches from one end of the day to the other. Sure I'm too ould a buck to marry anyway. I'd collapse if I got a grueller in the first buckle. My eyes'd close and my knees'd buckle. Could you imagine me after a honeymoon with my body black and blue and my tongue hangin' out? I can see her comin' after me *(Protects himself)* lookin' for more, game to the tail with a glint in her eye and me a dead duck on the flat o' my back. I wouldn't last as long as a hailstone in a hot fryin' pan. Cripes, Nellie, if you see me making for matrimony will you notify the undertaker?

Nellie: It's no good, Dad. It's no good at all, I'd only be depressin' you. Don't you know what old maids are like in a house? And worse I'd be gettin' as I got older.

Morisheen: Not with me, you wouldn't. I was down the river last winter and I saw a long-legged crane trying to break the ice to get a drink. Up comes a sparra, 'Anything doin'?' sez he to the crane. 'No good', sez the crane. 'Ah,' sez the sparra, 'we didn't drink enough of it while we had it.'

(From the distance discordant yells and shouts are heard – growing louder.)

'Tis them two lunatics that were here last night!

(Cries of 'Up Cuas!' and 'To hell with Bealabawn!' Enter Pakey followed by Petey.)

Pakey: Where's Daigan and Padraic?

Petey: Where's Padraic and Daigan?

Morisheen: They're not here.

Petey: The water is down in the Shannon an' the lad with the boat said he'd be chargin' double time from this on.

Pakey: Double time. Good God, that's twice the price! 'Tis daylight robbery.

Morisheen: And he should get danger money too!

Pakey: Why?

Petey: Why so?

Morisheen: For transporting a cargo of certified eejits like the two of you.

Nellie: Sit down and have a cup of tea before ye start.

Pakey: No, thanks. I'm after two huge cuts o' seed cake an ould woman gave me an' a fine saucepan o' new milk an' Petey here went home with a schoolmaster's daughter to a three-storey-high house an' they gave him bacon an' eggs an' what clsc was it, Pctcy?

Petey: Stuffed tomatoes an' them small knobs o' tender scones an' the schoolmaster invited me over for the pattern on the fifteenth of August.

Morisheen: And do you know why he invited you? Did he explain it to you?

Petey: No.

Morisheen: He wasn't fair now when he never told you why he invited you.

Petey: Why so?

Pakey: Why so?

Petey: Why so did he invite me?

Morisheen: The place do be black with people that day an' make a fortune chargin' people to have a look at you.

Pakey: Come on away Petey. This oul' fellow is always coddin' us.

Morisheen: Go easy a minute. What way did the fight go last night?

Pakey: Padraic O'Dea got the razz.

Petey: He got it all right. Talk about shoein' a wheel … He got at least forty flamin' licks into the kisser an' as many more on top o' the sconce.

Pakey: He got the stuffin' knocked out o' him in a fair fight. They were at it nearly half an hour but Jim Flynn was too quick for him.

Petey: 'Twas the first time I ever saw Padraic O'Dea capsized.

Morisheen: Where did he go after?

Petey: Don't you know the way fellas like that do be? We left him there grindin' his teeth an' cuttin' his tongue and cryin' to himself an' thinkin' of all the wrongs the world did him from the day he was born. That's the way fellas like that do be.

Pakey: That's the way fellas like that do be all right.

Morisheen: Well, Padraic isn't here now but Daigan went lookin' for him. We'll send them to the boat as soon as they turn up. Don't go without them. Are all the dancers gone home?

Pakey: They're all gone. We left one fella from Kilkee below doin' the Hokey Pokey.

Nellie: Have one mouthful o' tea.

Pakey: We haven't time. We're under orders from the fella that owns the boat to round up all the lads. We've them all contacted now except Padraic and Daigan and Cooney the corner forward.

Morisheen: Who's he?

Pakey: Yirra, Cooney, the corner forward. He was in Listowel last night. He was to follow us on. We couldn't be waitin' for him.

Petey: The last time I saw him he was sitting down at a table with a blondie-haired one from Listowel. Chips an' sausages he was eatin' and the blondie one had a big plate o' them sticky buns in front of her. 'Tis nearly ten miles of a rough road to Listowel.

Morisheen: He won't feel it … He'll have light pockets after the blonde.

Pakey: We'll be off. That fellow's asleep in some hayshed.

Petey: Maybe stuck in a hole in a ditch, drowned or well colonised with common fleas under a rick.

Nellie: Listen ... take a couple o' slices o' bacon with ye in case the hunger catches ye.

Pakey: Is it lean or fat or streaky?

Morisheen: Streaky.

                   (Nellie cuts a few slices of bacon)

Petey: Is it sweet?

Morisheen: As sweet as the breast of a Duhallow drake.

                   (Nellie hands them the bacon)

Pakey: God bless your hands!

                   (Immediately they stuff their mouths with bacon)

Petey: 'Tis nicely tasting.

Pakey: Up Cuas!

Petey: Up Cuas! *(They both yell and whoop)*

Pakey: Down Bealabawn!

Petey: To hell with Bealabawn!

                   (Both yelling, exit)

Morisheen: Cracked as the crows! You can't whack the youth.

Nellie: I didn't know there was a fight last night. What started it?

Morisheen: They were crowning a new king. A young fellow called Flynn played well yesterday, and there was a girl here last night. 'Twas inevitable.

Nellie: Did he get a bad beating?

Morisheen: I'm afraid so. You'd be a long while getting the better of a man like him.

Nellie: Maybe he's thrown down unconscious somewhere. Should we look for him?

Morisheen: Padraic is a man who will have to advance up to himself to be reckernised before he ruins himself. Sometimes a man needs to talk to himself. Best let him be.

(Enter Daigan, alarmed)

Daigan: He didn't show?

Morisheen: No.

Daigan: An' where would he be gone? *(He goes to door and calls)* Padraic! ... *(Exiting, calls)* Padraic! ... Padraic! ... *(Exits distractedly)*

(Nellie pours a cup of tea)

Morisheen: Well 'twas a full night an' mornin'. What Daigan said meant nothin' at all. You're pleasant-lookin' an' easy to get along with. Sure a body would never know you'd be in the house, you're so quiet. You're clean and tidy and your feedin' is fit for the Pope o' Rome.

Nellie: You never give up tryin'! You won't have to be trying for long more for my sake.

(A figure appears at the door – Padraic O'Dea. He is obviously at the end of his tether)

Morisheen: Padraic ... Padraic ... Good God, man, you're done in completely. Where were you?

(Morisheen and Nellie rise hastily to assist him – they lead him to a chair. Nellie hurries to a cupboard and gets a small bowl which she places on table)

Nellie: *(Searching drawer of cupboard)* Lint! ... Lint! ... Where's the Lint?

Morisheen: You're a sight, man!

Nellie:	Ah, thank God, here it is.

(Finds scissors cuts square – places it in bowl, fetches kettle and pours water into bowl. Morisheen is kneeling, feeling Padraic's face and cuts)

Morisheen: You took a frightful hammerin'!

Padraic: 'Twasn't the beatin' so much. I've gone through my own Gethsemane this night.

Morisheen: Ah, I know! ... I know! ... God help us. I know well what 'twas like with you.

Padraic: Sorry to be such a nuisance! ... Where's Daigan?

Morisheen: He's gone searchin' for you ... the man is distracted worrying about you.

Padraic: If he found me like this I'd have choked him.

Nellie: You have great healin'. Your cuts are closed an' there's no infection.

Padraic: I dipped my head in a pool o' salt-water an' held it under till I nearly suffocated. I did that twenty times if I did it once because my head was openin' and splittin' with concussion. I don't know what got into me then because I stripped off my clothes an' went out into the sea up to my neck and I stood there and let the hands of the tide search me and I let the small waves wash over my body because I was sore and there was an ache in every part o' me.

Morisheen: You had a rough night, boy.

Padraic: I rose out o' the water then an' drew my clothes on me an' stole up to the side of the barn where the dancin' was an' I peeped in through a crack in the wall an' there they were inside dancin' an' singin' an' huggin' an' I might be dead for all they knew an' you'd swear that a man of my mettle never suffered a defeat that night because the crowd inside were conductin' themselves the same as if nothin' happened an' I said to myself, 'Does anyone want me or what is it that's in me that makes me stay outside the crowd an' be a black stranger to people I've known all my life?'

Morisheen: Every man is a stranger to his neighbour and the nearer the neighbour, the bigger the stranger. It's only an act, all this good-fellowship an' back-slappin' an' hand-shakin' an' praisin'. No one means it in earnest. It's the thing to do. A man must stand alone while he's findin' himself.

Padraic: I'll have to be goin'. The boat will be waitin' an' the water is fit for crossin'. *(He tries weakly to rise but they restrain him.)* I'm fagged out.

Morisheen: Go to bed for an hour or two an' I'll think o' some plan to delay the boat. You don't want to be seen in that state.

Padraic: *(Swelling)* What do I care about them? What do I give a hang about any of them?

Morisheen: The spirit is in you all the time. You'll never lose that ... but you must get it into your head you lost the fight.

Padraic: I'm getting it into my head thro' all the sneaky entrances I know.

Nellie: Go to my bed for an hour. It's soft an' it's warm an' it's at the back o' the house where you'll not be disturbed.

Padraic: No ... thanks all the same ... If I went to sleep now I wouldn't wake for a month. I'll be all right.

Nellie: I'll get a cup o' tea for you.

Morisheen: An' I'll put a lacer o' the hot stuff in it.

Padraic: No hot stuff ... Sundays an' Holy Days only! ... I thought a lot of things an' I out there up to my neck in water. I can walk across now to Clare, I said to myself and before I'm gone a hundred feet my worries in this world'll be over.

Morisheen: A natural thought considerin' the circumstances.

(Nellie hands Padraic a cup of tea)

Padraic: But a strange thing, I thought about you.

(Nellie turns away. Padraic looks into the distance)

Padraic: I thought about the little talk we had last night and I said to myself, now don't laugh at me, that girl had pure eyes and eyes as clear as the green ice of winter where eagles fly ... Don't laugh at me for the love of God.

(Morisheen slides discreetly towards room – Nellie stands with her back turned to Padraic – Padraic rises and addresses her)

Padraic: Don't laugh at me for the love o' God, whatever else, because that's one thing I couldn't stand.

Nellie: *(Without turning)* I won't laugh at you. That's one thing you can be sure of. But that's all I'll promise you because you'll be goin' away for good to Clare in a short while and you'll have forgotten whatever you're likely to say by tomorrow.

Padraic: That's where you're wrong, if you knew me you'd know I was never a man for idle talk. I say what I mean and I never say anythin' easily an' maybe that's my trouble. That's the kind o' man I am.

(Enter Daigan)

Daigan: Thank God! ... Thank God! ... You're fine ... you're grand. I didn't know what happened to you. 'Tis great to see you. 'Tis new life to me to see you. New life, man.

(Padraic is not even aware of his existence)

Look Padraic ... look ... you stay here as long as you want an' I'll go down an' hold the boat ... don't be in a hurry, they won't go without you ... an' lookit, if you're goin' to be talkin' to that girl tell her that I'm sorry deep down in the bottom of my heart for hurtin' her an' if you're fond of her, tell her I'll be fond of her too.

(Exit Daigan)

Padraic: Can you hear me, Nellie? ... I'm tellin' you that I care for you ... I really care for you ... I feel so deeply for you that words are a waste. I know myself and I know that you're the woman for me. That's all I can tell you for now and it's the only way I know how to tell you. Would you marry me soon an' come back to Clare with me? *(He goes near her and puts his hands on her shoulders, she is still turned away from him)* You'll like it over in Cuas an' you'll be happy because I'll make you happy an' I'll work mornin', noon an' night for your happiness.

(Slowly Nellie turns and faces him)

Nellie: No Padraic. It's no good ... You don't love me ... Go back to Clare and marry a good-lookin' girl that you might have real passion for. It's some kind of pity you feel, and pity is not what I want an' it wouldn't be any good for you either. Take your stuff an' go now because I'm goin' to cry in a minute an' I'll be a terrible sight because there's that many years o' tears inside o' me I'd frighten you an' I don't want you to go away with greater pity for me.

Padraic: What am I goin' to say to you or what honest way can a man express himself when he wants to pour out the real feelings of his heart? I can't say I love you. I wouldn't understand what I'd be saying myself if I did.

Nellie: Say no more only go now, because every word you say is hurtin' me more an' more an' if you don't go quick I'll have to run away an' hide myself. I'm serious too an' I can't listen to you any more. Go, go on away to the boat an' don't have the neighbours laughin' at me, so if you have any small spatter of the compassion you say you have you'll turn on your heel an' go out that door now this minute.

Padraic: If I said Nellie, 'I love you', it would mean only three words. Anyone can say them. Anyone can say 'I love you' ... I can't. It would mean nothin' to me but I know I can give you a lifetime of labour an' I'll give you the strength o' my shoulders and my body an' all the power that's in me to cater for you, Nellie Brick. I don't know whether that's love or not but that's what I want to do for you. *(Lifts her aloft)* I want to twirl you like a spinning top and stop you from spinning slowly, to know every bit of you.

Nellie:	You mean it Padraic ... you really mean it?

Padraic: I never felt for anyone what I feel for you. It's broken in me whatever it was that damned up my natural feelings.

(They embrace)

Nellie: O, Padraic, my Padraic ... my dear, dear Padraic. What will we do, what will I do about you?

Padraic: I'll come for you at the first low tide in September an' we'll be married. I can't do anything before that because I have to settle a pile of things first, in Cuas.

Nellie: I'll be waitin' for you at the low tide.

(They embrace again)

Padraic: Do you know the pier at Cuas? Did you ever spot it across the water?

Nellie: I often saw it of a fine mornin'.

(Padraic puts his hands around her waist and they stand in the doorway)

Padraic: Look, *(Points)* look now apast my hand, well to the left. It's the third whitewashed house over the harbour to the sea side of the pier. Do you see it?

Nellie: Is that it! I often noticed that house when I was a child and I wondered what kind of strange people lived there.

Padraic: I used to look across here often when I was young in summertime, an' there used to be a blue haze mindin' the low hills here at this side o' the Shannon. Did you ever feel a great loneliness when you see a crooked wall of low hills in the distance and silver so plentiful on the water between, that there wouldn't be any cure for your loneliness unless there was someone you could tell your feelin's to?

Nellie: I know … I know better than anybody … Oh, look at them two, it's Pakey and Petey an' what's that they have between them? He's like he'd be dead an' here's the crowd from the boat followin' them.

Padraic: *(Joining Nellie in laughter)* That's Cooney, the corner forward.

Nellie: Is he drunk or what?

                 (They withdraw into the kitchen from the doorway)

Padraic: I'll be off with them shortly. 'Twon't be long, a few weeks an' I'll be back.

                 (Sound of music comes nearer. Pakey and Petey enter, supporting Cooney)

Pakey: High and low we searched, hither and over. At first we thought he was drowned but then we heard the snores.

Petey: He's still sound … We found him asleep in a boggy field in the middle of a herd o' donkeys.

                 (Pakey intones like donkey into Cooney's ear, who sleeps on undisturbed. Enter Frank followed by Daigan, Jim and others)

Frank: We're all here now. Come on down to the boat let ye! We'll march down to the boat the same as if we were never beaten.

Cooney: We'll rise again.

                 (Enter Morisheen)

Morisheen: 'Twill be our turn to cross to Clare next year.

Pakey: We'll give ye a hot reception.

Petey: We'll murder 'em!

Pakey: Glory Cuas!

Petey: Down with Bealabawn!

              (Frank, after an initial note, breaks into a march)

Padraic: Morisheen ... the next time you'll see me, I'll be wanting
              the hand of your daughter.

Morisheen: *(Aloud jubilantly)* I always knew it! I always knew it! 'A
              man with grey hair will be hailed along the four shores of
              Ireland. This man will come into his own after years of
              torment and misery. This man will have the heart of a cock
              blackbird for he shall sit on the crown of a sidecar in the
              streets of Killarney. A woman with a supple frame an' a
              shinin' eye will ride by his side and break the heart of a
              certain postman in Cockatoo Lane. His son will rise up to
              coward the country. This man will be pampered and spoiled
              by the woman of his choosing and, lo and behold, the name
              of this man shall by Morisheen Brick'. *(Swings his thumbs
              around and points to himself)*

              (All cheer and applaud)

Padraic: Your prophecy came true in the end, Morisheen Brick.
              Thank God for that.

Nellie: *(Takes Padraic's hand)* The first low tide in September.

Padraic: The first low tide.

Morisheen: You brought nothing but goodness here; may God go with
              you my lovely man from Clare! May God go with you all!

              *(Meanwhile all the Clare footballers have gathered at either
              side of the banner. At Daigan's command they mark time,
              including Cooney. Then, marching time slowly, they sing)*

Footballers: Alas now for the men of Cuas
              Again we've lost the fray
              Though hopes arc dashed and fortunes crashed
              We'll fight another day
              Cuas men crossed, Cuas men tossed
              It matters not who won or lost
              Cuas, Cuas, Cuas,

Cuas, Cuas, Cuas,
What matters is to play the game.

(Then the marching of time ceases. They stand erect. Padraic kisses Nellie farewell and marches away with the team as all sing.)

All: Steady now the men of Cuas
Before the breaking day
Our tide is high, a last goodbye
Before we sail away
Cuas boys here, Cuas boys there
Cuas boys, Cuas boys everywhere
Cuas, Cuas, Cuas,
Cuas, Cuas, Cuas,
The men of Cuas are always there.

(Final Curtain)

The Men of Cuas

Words and music: John B. Keane
Arrangement: James N. Healy

1. Glo- ry to the men of Cuas, the pride of the Coun-ty Clare In the rough or
6. on the loose The Cuas boys will be there. Cuas boys here, Cuas boys there Cuas boys Cuas boys
12. everywhere, Cuas, Cuas Cuas, Cuas, Cuas Cuas, The men of Cuas are al-ways there.

The Men of Cuas

Glory to the men of Cuas
The pride of the County Clare
In the rough or on the loose
The Cuas boys will be there.
Cuas boys here, Cuas boys there
Cuas boys, Cuas boys everywhere.
Cuas, Cuas, Cuas,
Cuas, Cuas, Cuas,
The men of Cuas are always there.

GLOSSARY

A chroide = my love
Agaidh fidil = mask for wren day
Amadán = fool
Bán = white
Bart = bundle
Bollav = dumb
Bonham [banbh] = piglet
Collop = leg
Dia linn = God be with us
Disase = Disease
Draiodheacht = druidism
Dúchas = heritage
Fionnán = coarse moor grass
Flitch = chunk
Fostooks = stack
Gábhail = amount/armful
Gaiscíoch = warrior/hero
Gamalóg = silly
Gattled = mounted
Gearrcach = infant
Geowckacks = young bird, fledgling
Grádhmar = loving
Heidle fo peeb = spirit behind pipe music
Horse blocker = dealer
Male = meal
M'anam an diabhail = my soul for the devil
Mo chroí = my heart
Olagón = wailing
Pilibín = plover
Pizawn [piseán] = withered pea
Pucking = hitting
Ropaire = villain/scoundral
Síofra = sprite
Sleen of turf = spade
Spailpín = travelling workman
Tamaill = short time
Triopall = cluster/bunch
Wilent = violent
Yalla = yellow